The Manifold Wisdom of God Seen in Covenant Theology
By George Walker

The Manifold Wisdom of God Seen in Covenant Theology
By George Walker

Edited and updated by C. Matthew McMahon and Therese B. McMahon
Transcribed by Beth Saathoff

Published by Puritan Publications
A Ministry of A Puritan's Mind
4101 Coral Tree Circle #214
Coconut Creek, FL 33073
www.puritanshop.com
www.apuritansmind.com
www.puritanpublications.com

This Hardback First Edition, 2012
Electronic Edition, 2012
Manufactured in the United States of America

ISBN: 978-1-938721-25-0
eISBN: 978-1-938721-24-3

MEET GEORGE WALKER

George Walker (1581-1651), puritan divine, born about 1581 at Hawkshead in Furness, Lancashire, was educated at the Hawkshead grammar school, founded by his kinsman, Archbishop Edwin Sandys. He was a near relative of John Walker (d. 1588). Fuller states that George Walker "being visited when a child with the small-pox, and the standers-by expecting his dissolution, he started up out of a trance with this ejaculation, "Lord, take me not away till I have showed forth thy praise," which made his parents devote him to the ministry after his recovery." He went to St. John's College, Cambridge, where he graduated with a B.A. in 1608 and an M.A. in 1611. His former tutor, Christopher Foster, who held the rectory of St. John Evangelist, Watling Street, the smallest parish in London, resigned that benefice in favor of Walker, who was inducted on April 29, 1614 on the presentation of the dean and chapter of Canterbury Cathedral (Hennessy, Nov. Report. Eccl. p. 310). There he continued all his life, refusing higher preferment often proffered him. In 1614 he accused Anthony Wotton of Socinian heresy and blasphemy. This led to a "conference before eight learned divines," which ended in a vindication of Wotton. On March 2, 1618-19 he was appointed chaplain to Nicholas Felton, bishop of Ely. He was already esteemed an excellent logician, hebraist, and divine, and readily engaged in disputes with "heretics" and "papists." On July 10, 1621 he was incorporated with a B.D. of Oxford.

On May 31, 1623 he had a disputation on the authority of the church with Sylvester Norris, who called himself Smith. An account of this was published in the following year under the title of "The Summe of a Disputation between Mr. Walker...and a Popish Priest, calling himselfe Mr. Smith." About the same time Walker was associated with Dr. Daniel Featley in a disputation with Father John Fisher (real name Percy), and afterwards published "Fisher's Folly Unfolded; or the Vaunting Jesuites Vanity discovered in a Challenge of his...undertaken and answered by George Walker," 1624, 4to. On March 11, 1633-4 he undertook to contribute 20s. yearly for five years towards the repair of St. Paul's (Cal. State Papers, Dom. 1633-4, p. 498). His puritanism was displeasing to Laud, who in 1636 mentions him in his yearly report to Charles I as one "who had all his time been but a disorderly and peevish man, and now of late hath very frowardly preached against the Lord Bishop of Ely [White] his book concerning the Lord's Day, set out by authority; but upon a canonical admonition given him to desist he hath recollected himself, and I hope will be advised," (Laud, Troubles and Tryal, 1695, p. 536). In 1638 appeared his "Doctrine of the Sabbath," which bears the imprint of Amsterdam, and contains extreme and peculiar views of the sanctity of the Lord's Day. A second edition, entitled "The Holy Weekly Sabbath," was printed in 1641. His main hypothesis was refuted by H. Witsius in his "De Oeconomia Foederum," 1694.

Walker was committed to prison on Nov. 11, 1638 for some "things tending to faction and disobedience to authority" found in a sermon delivered by him on the 4th of the same month (Cal. State Papers, Dom. 1658-9, p. 98). His case was introduced into the House of Commons on May 20, 1641, and his imprisonment declared illegal. He was afterwards restored to his parsonage, and received other compensation for his losses. At the trial of Laud in 1643 the imprisonment of Walker was made one of the charges against the archbishop (Laud, Troubles, p. 237). When he was free again he became very busy as a preacher and author. Four of his works are dated 1641: 1. God made visible in His Works, or a Treatise on the Eternal Works of God. 2. A Disputation between Master Walker and a Jesuite in the House of one Thomas Bates, in Bishop's Court in the Old Bailey, concerning the Ecclesiastical Function. 3. The Key of Saving Knowledge. 4. Socinianisme in the Fundamental Point of Justification discovered and confuted. In the last, which was directed against John Goodwin, he revived his coarse imputations against Wotton, who found a vindicator in Thomas Gataker, in his "Mr. Anthony Wotton's Defence against Mr. George Walker's Charge," Cambridge. 1641, 12mo. In the following year Walker replied in "A True Relation of the Chiefe Passages between Mr. Anthony Wotton and Mr. George Walker." Goodwin in his "Treatise on Justification," 1642, deals with the various doctrinal points raised by Walker.

Walker joined the *Westminster Assembly of Divines* in 1643, in the records of which body his name often appears as that of an active and influential member. On Jan. 29, 1644-5 he preached a fast-day sermon before the House of Commons, which was shortly afterwards published, with an "Epistle" giving some particulars of his imprisonment. In the same year (1646) he printed "A Brotherly and Friendly Censure of the Errour of a Dead Friend and Brother in Christian Affection." This refers to some utterance of W. Prynne. On Sept. 26, 1645 parliament appointed him a 'trier' of elders in the London classis. There is an interesting undated tract by him entitled "An Exhortation to Dearely beloved countrimen, all the Natives of the Countie of Lancaster, inhabiting in and about the Citie of London, tending to persuade and stirre them up to a yearely contribution for the erection of Lectures, and maintaining of some Godly and Painfull Preachers in such places of that Country as have most neede." He himself did his share in the direction indicated, for, in addition to spending other sums in Lancashire, he allowed the minister of Hawkshead 20l. a year, and the parsonage-house and glebe there were long called "Walker Ground," from their being his gift. He was also a benefactor to Sion College library and a liberal supporter of the assembly of divines.

Wood justly styles Walker a "severe partisan," but he was also as Fuller said, "a man of an holy life, humble heart, and bountiful hand."

He died in his seventieth year in 1651, and was buried in his church in Watling Street, which was destroyed in the fire of 1666.

The works of George Walker:

1. *Ernsthaffte*...Representation des Urtheils des Ministerii in der Provintz Londen, etc. [Signed T. Gatakeri, G. Walker, etc.] 4to. 1649.

2. *A Brotherly and Friendly Censure of the errour of a dear friend and brother in Christian affection [W. Prynne] in answer to his four Questions [concerning Exommunication and Suspension from the Sacrament] lately sent abroad, etc.* 4to. pp. 10. 1645.

3. *The Doctrine of the Sabbath.* Wherein the first institution of the weekly Sabbath, with the time thereof, the nature of the Law binding men to keep it,...are laid open and proved out of the Holy Scriptures...Delivered in divers sermons by G. W. 4to. pp. 167. Amsterdam, 1638.

4. *An Exhortation for contributions to maintain Teachers in Lancashire*, circa 1641 . . . With an introduction by Charles W. Sutton. [in Chetham Remains, N.S. vol. 47. Chetham Miscellanies. N. S. vol. 1] 4to. pp. xiii. 25.

5. *Fisher's Folly Unfolded*; or, The Vaunting Jesuites Vanity discovered in a challenge of his (by him proudly made, but on his part poorely performed). Undertaken and answered by G. W. London, 1624.

6. *God made Visible in His Workes*, or a Treatise of the Externall Workes of God, etc. London, 1641.

7. *The History of the Creation*, as it is written by Moses in the first and second Chapters of Genesis, plainly opened and expounded in several sermons preache in London. Whereunto is added a short Treatise of Gods actuall Providence, in ruling, ordering, and governing the world and all things therein. London, 1641.

8. *The Key of Saving Knowledge*, opening out of the Holy Scriptures, the right way, and straight passages to Eternal life. Or, a dialogue wherein the chiefe principles of Christian Religion are unfolded, etc. 8vo. London, 1641.

9. *The Manifold Wisdom of God Seen in Covenant Theology*; in the divers dispensations of Grace by Jesus Christ. In the Old and New Testaments. Their agreement and difference. London, 1640.

10. *A Sermon preached from Psalm 58:9.* before the House of Commons at their late solemne monthly fast, Jan. 29. 1644. 4to. pp. 53. London, 1645.

11. *Socinianisme in the Fundamentall Point of Justification Discovered and Confuted.* Or, an answer to a written pamphlet maintaining that faith is in a proper sense without a trope imputed to Beleevers in justification, *etc.* 8vo. pp. 355. London, 1641.

12. *The Summe of a Disputation between Mr Walker, Pastor of St. John the Evangelist in Watling-Street, and a Popish Priest, calling himself Mr Smith, but indeed Norrice, assisted by some other Priests and Papists.* Held in the presence of some worthy knights; with other gentlemen of both religions. 4to. [London?] 1624.

13. *A True Copie of the disputation held between Master Walker and a Jesuite,* in the house of one Thomas Bates in Bishops Court in the Old Baily, concerning ecclesiastical function. London, 1641.

14. *A True Relation of the chiefe passages between Mr. Anthony Wotton, and Mr. George Walker, in the yeare of our Lord 1611 and in the yeares next following untill 1615.* Written by George Walker, out of his owne papers which he hath yet to shew; for the vindicating of himselfe from some imputations laid on him by Mr. Thomas Gataker, in his defence of Mr. Wotton. 4to. London, 1642.

15. *Held in the presence of two Worthy Knights, and of a few other Gentlement, some Catholikes, some Protestants. With a briefe Confutation of the false and adulterated summe, which M. Walker...hath divulged of the same.* 4to. 1624.

For Further Study:

[Fuller's *Worthies*; Wood's *Fasti*, i. 399, ed. Bliss; Newcourt's *Repartorium*, i. 375; Ward's *Gresham Professors*, p. 40; Dodd's *Church History*, 1739, pp. 394, 402; Neal's *Puritans*, 2nd edit. ii. 416; Brook's *Puritans*, ii. 347 ; House of Commons' *Journals*, ii. 151, 201, 209, iv. 288, 346; House of Lord's *Journals*, iv. 214, 457, vi. 469 ; *Hist.. MSS. Comm.* 8th Rep. App. p. 170; Jackson's *Life of John Goodwin*, 2nd edit. 1872, p. 38; Gastrell's *Notitia Cestriensis* (Chetham Soc.), ii. 519; Cox's *Literature of the Sabbath Question*, 1853; Mitchell and Struthers's *Minutes of the Westminster Assembly*, 1874; Mitchell's *Westminster Assembly*, 1874; Hennessy's *Novum Repertorium.* p. 310.]

[Taken in part from the public domain *National Dictionary of Biography*.]

Table of Contents

MEET GEORGE WALKER 3

Original Title Page 12

THE STATIONER TO THE READER 13

OVERVIEW OF THE WORK 14

CHAPTER 1: INTRODUCTION...20

CHAPTER 2: THE WORD TESTAMENT 26

CHAPTER 3: A TWO-FOLD USE 32

CHAPTER 4: COVENANT 45

CHAPTER 5: TYPES OF COVENANTS 53

CHAPTER 6: THE COVENANT OF GRACE 60

CHAPTER 7: THE COVENANT OF GRACE AND THE GOSPEL 71

CHAPTER 8: AGREEMENT OF THE COVENANTS............ 81

CHAPTER 9: A THREE-FOLD AGREEMENT 83

CHAPTER 10: DIFFERENCES.. 85

CHAPTER 11: USE OF THE DOCTRINE 93

CHAPTER 12: AGREEMENT IN THE OLD TESTAMENT . 96

CHAPTER 13: SEVEN DIFFERENCES 103

CHAPTER 14: TWO-FOLD USE 111

CHAPTER 15: THE COVENANT WITH MOSES 115

CHAPTER 16: A PURE AND MIXED COVENANT 119

CHAPTER 17: GOD'S PROVIDENCE.............................135

CHAPTER 18: THE LAW AND THE GOSPEL....................139

[Original Title Page]

THE
MANIFOLD
WISDOM
OF GOD:

*In the Diverse Dispensation
of Grace by Jesus Christ*

In the Old and New Testament

In the covenant of Faith and Works

With their Agreement and Differences.

BY GEORGE WALKER
Westminster Divine

LONDON,
Printed by R.H. for *John Bartlett*, and are to be fold at the sign
of the Gilt Cop, near S. *Austin's* Gate in *Paul's* Churchyard.
1640.

THE STATIONER TO THE READER

Christian reader, this brief treatise being written twenty-four years ago, for the benefit of private Christians (who were not content with hearing once of the subject when it was publicly preached, and desired a copy in writing) was imparted by the author, as to some of his hearers, so to various preachers, who on the report of others were very much moved to desire its sight. After it had passed through many hands, it was brought to me, by one who judging it profitable, and fit to be communicated to many, commended the publishing of it to me; which I presumed might be done without any wrong to the author, being sent forth from hand to hand by himself, neither under his own, nor any other's name. If the work commends itself and finds approbation, I shall be encouraged to inquire and seek after other works of the same author, who as I hear have written in fair manuscript various treatises concerning several necessary heads of divinity, and chief principles of religion. Take this in good part in the meanwhile, and if greater works follow, by which God's people may be edified in faith and knowledge, give God the glory.

To whose grace I commend thee now and forever.

J.B.

OVERVIEW OF THE WORK

CHAPTER 1

The great profit and benefit which arises from the knowledge of the true difference between the Old and New Testament is the Covenant of Works and the Covenant of Grace; the Law and the Gospel.

CHAPTER 2

What the word *testament* signifies, and what is the nature of a testament. That the Scriptures both of the Old and New Testament are called *testaments* only in respect to Christ, who by his death ratified them, and not in respect of God the Father, who could not die to make them in force. The agreement and difference between the Old and New Testament are plainly shown.

CHAPTER 3

The doctrine of the former chapter is applied by way of use, to confute five differences which the schoolmen have made, and three differences which the Jesuits have added to them, between the Old and New Testament, and their vanity is discovered by this, and a two-fold use is moreover shown.

CHAPTER 4

What the word *covenant* signifies, what is the nature of a covenant in general.

CHAPTER 5

The several kinds of covenants between God and men. The Covenant of Nature is described. The Covenant of Grace is unfolded, and the blessings in it promised are rehearsed. That this covenant is a covenant of free grace is plainly proved. The division of it into the Old and New Covenant.

CHAPTER 6

The Covenant of Grace first made with Adam after his fall. The liberty by it given to man proves that we gain more by Christ then we lost in Adam. Of the renewing of it with Noah. The forces of renewing it with Abraham, and revealing it more plainly by seven things. Of the renewing of it with Israel and Mount Sinai and by Moses. That it is called the Old Covenant in respect of the New Covenant in the Gospel. That it is mixed of the Covenant of Works and of the Covenant of Grace. The reasons why God is making it did renew the Covenant of Works, and mingle it with the Covenant of Grace made with man in Christ after his fall.

CHAPTER 7

Of the New Covenant of Grace, as it is made most plainly in the Gospel, and in the New Testament. The reasons why it is called the *New Covenant*.

CHAPTER 8

The method and order propounded, which is to be followed in showing how the New and Old Covenants of Grace agree and differ.

CHAPTER 9

The three-fold agreement between the Covenant of Nature, which is called the first covenant, and the Covenant of Grace, which is called the second covenant.

CHAPTER 10

The six notable things in which the Covenant of Nature differs from the Covenant of Grace.

CHAPTER 11

The profitable and holy use which may be made of the doctrine concerning those differences between the Covenant of Nature and the Covenant of Grace.

CHAPTER 12

The six-fold agreement between the Covenant of Grace, as it was revealed to the fathers of the Old Testament, and the same renewed and more fully explained in the Gospel.

CHAPTER 13

The seven-fold differences between the Covenant of Grace, as it was made with the fathers, and the covenant as it was made in the Gospel.

CHAPTER 14

A two-fold use is made of the doctrine in the two former chapters.

CHAPTER 15

The agreement between the pure and plain Covenant of Grace in the Gospel, and the mixed covenant which God made with Israel on Mount Horeb, by the ministry of Moses, which consisted partly of the Covenant of Works, and partly the Covenant of Grace.

CHAPTER 16

The several differences between the pure and mixed covenant.

CHAPTER 17

The use of the doctrine is shown for the discovering of God's singular providence in preparing means of grace fit for the several ages of the world.

CHAPTER 18

The signification of the words, *Law* and *Gospel*. How they agree and differ, being taken in their several senses. Finally, the use of the doctrine.

July 30, 1640.

[*original*] Imprimatur,

The Wykes.

CHAPTER 1:

INTRODUCTION

A brief treatise concerning the agreement and difference between the Old and New Testaments; the first covenant between God and man, in innocency, which is the old Covenant of Works and the New Covenant made with mankind, in Christ, which is called the covenant of Free Grace; also between the Law and Gospel.

It is an ancient custom which has been for many ages in use among the learned before their entrance into the large exposition of the Gospel of Christ in the New Testament, to premise and lay down by way of preparation, the nature, difference, and agreement between the Old and New Testament, the Covenant of Works, and the Covenant of Grace, the Law and the Gospel, the prophets and evangelists. Surely if we rightly consider the end and use of this practice, and the profit and benefit which may arise from the knowledge of the nature of these beforehand, and of the true difference and agreement between them, we cannot but judge those learned men worthy of imitation. It will be profitable for us to walk in the same steps, when the same occasion is offered. For the knowledge of the true difference of the Old and New Testament, the Covenant of Works, and the Covenant of Grace, the Law, and the Gospel, will not only give us good light, for the right understanding of various particular speeches used in the New Testament by the evangelists and apostles, but also may keep us from many dangerous errors, and enable us to answer the objections of the adversaries which they make out of the words of the apostles and prophets, wrongfully wrested and misconstrued according to their own foolish imaginations. As for example, sometimes the apostles exhort us to observe the things which by tradition have been delivered to us, and command to observe the good orders and ordinances established in the churches. Now a man not knowing the difference between the Old and New Testament, the Law and the Gospel, when he hears such speeches, may imagine that in those words he is enjoined to observe the traditions and ordinances of *Moses*, and so may with the seduced *Galatians* fall into a great error. So in some places of the apostles we read, that "they who are born of God sin not, that they who sin are of the devil," (1 John 3:8-9), that "they who sin willfully after that they have received the knowledge of the truth, can have no sacrifice for their sin," (Heb. 10:26), and that "he who believeth not is condemned already," (John 3:18).

These things when a man hears or reads, who is ignorant of the difference between the Law and the Gospel, may imagine with our new upstart heretics, that every sin which a man willingly commits, proves him to be a child of the devil, destitute of all grace, and that when men are once called and justified, they cannot willingly sin any more. And many such errors he may run into. But if he understands that sin in those places signifies sin against the evangelical Law, the two commandments of the Gospel which commands us to believe and repent, and not every sin against any commandments of the Law, he cannot be deceived. For sin against the Gospel is when a man being called before to believe and profess the Gospel, and having received the its commandments, which enjoin repentance of all sin, and belief in Jesus Christ whom the Gospel preaches, afterwards rebels against these two precepts, that is, falls into infidelity and impenitency, which is *willful apostasy*. Now these sins no one can commit who is born of God, or has any true saving grace in him; and if we so understand sin, we shall not be deceived. So likewise the evangelists and apostles tell us that if we do such and such good works we are righteous, if "we call on the name of the Lord we shall be saved," (Acts 2:21); and our Savior says that he will pronounce them the blessed of his Father, and will say to them, "Come, inherit the kingdom: for ye fed me when I was hungry, and visited me in the prisons...In that ye did these things to my little ones," (Matt. 25:34-40). And again, "Many sins are forgiven her, for she loved much," (Luke 7:47). If we do not know the difference between the Law and the Gospel, we may by these speeches be moved to think that men are justified and saved by their works, and may merit heaven by good deed, as the Jews and papists believe. But if we know, that by good deeds and righteous works, the evangelist and apostles commonly mean not simple works of obedience to the Law, but works done by a true saving and justifying faith, he cannot be deceived. For such works have these two prerogatives above all others. First, in that they are fruits of a justifying faith, which can never fail, and proceed from the Spirit of regeneration, which makes us one with Christ, sons of God in him, and abides in us, as in immortal seed, they are infallible tokens of our justification, and assure to us the crown of glory which Christ has purchased for us, and the kingdom of heaven which is the inheritance of sons. And therefore we may truly say, that he which does such works is righteous, and shall be saved, and enjoy all blessedness, not meaning that they *make* him righteous or merit heaven; but that they are the *evidences* of his right to heaven. And the more they are, and the greater and more excellent, the more they testify a man's union and communion with Christ by a lively faith, and give more assurance of a greater reward. Secondly, being the works of a man that is justified by faith, and has perfect communion of Christ's righteousness, they have all their spots and stains cleansed and covered with the robe of Christ's righteousness, and all their defects by this supplied fully, and so they are perfect in righteous works, as well as the one who does them is a perfect righteous man, not in *themselves*, but by virtue of *Christ*, his obedience, which is *communicated* and *imputed* to the worker of them, and in him to them also. They are righteous, and are so called, not actually or effectually, but *passively*; that is not for making the doer righteous, but by the doer's receiving of Christ's righteousness by that faith in which they are fruits. This righteousness supplies all their defects, and makes them righteous, not by reason of a natural change in themselves, or alterations of their nature, but by spiritual communion which they have of it, together with the *doers* of them. So if we understand these words in the evangelical sense, we cannot be deceived, but may know the truth, and know how to answer all gainsayers. I could bring many instances of this nature, but these are sufficient to show that before we can sufficiently expound and rightly understand the Gospel, it is necessary that we should know, and be able to show the nature, and also the agreement and difference between the Law and the Gospel of Saint *John*, which I have undertaken. I will follow the steps of learned reformers of former times, and will endeavor to show briefly the agreement and difference between the Old and New Testament, between the old Covenant of Works, and the new Covenant of Grace, and between the Law and the Gospel in the first place. And in so doing I will labor to reform some things which they have done before and to handle this point a little more *distinctly*. For where the most part of them confusedly compare the Law and the Gospel together without distinction of the words, and while they labor to make the Gospel more glorious by all means, they do put *too great a difference* between it and the Law, which has been a cause of much error to many, and even of vilifying and contemning the Old Testament and the Law. My desire and purpose is, first to show the several acceptations and the true sense and meaning of the words; and then to declare the true agreement and difference, and to make those differences which are observed by others to agree together so far as truth will suffer, and to cut off all vain and needless differences. This doing I hope I shall reserve to each point their due reverence and respect. God shall have *his glory* by *both* the Law and Gospel. Your hearts shall be enabled with love of both, and you will be better enabled to understand the true meaning of the Gospel, and to feel the power of it in your souls.

CHAPTER 2:
THE WORD TESTAMENT

What the word testament signifies, and what is the nature of a testament. That the Scriptures both of the Old and New Testament are called testaments only in respect to Christ, who by his death ratified them, and not in respect of God the Father, who could not die to make them in force. The agreement and difference between the Old and New Testament are plainly shown.

First for the word *testament* signifies the last will of a man which he makes before his death, and leaves behind him either in word or writing, testified by seals and witnesses. He does this by virtue of that which will he dispose by his lands and possessions which he has purchased, and all his goods which he has gathered in his lifetime. And he bequeaths them as he wills, and to whom he thinks fit, either freely or with condition, to have and hold them after his death, and not before. This is the true and proper meaning of the word, and so it is used by the apostles, (*cf.* Heb. 9:16). And because the apostle there calls the covenant *Christ's testament*, and also elsewhere in his epistles wherever he speaks of the Old and

New Covenant, that is, of the covenant of the *Law* and of the *Gospel*, uses the Greek word διαθήκη (*diatheke*), even the same which there he uses for the *last will and testament* of a testator.

On this it comes to pass, that the books of the Law and the Prophets, before Christ, and the covenant in them are called the *Old Testament*, and that very fitly in some respect; I mean in respect of Christ the Mediator. For the truth is, that the Covenant of Grace more obscurely revealed to the fathers in the writings of the Law and Prophets, and more plainly in the Gospel and writings of the apostles, was never in force, or could be ratified but *by the death of Christ*. It was, before his coming, sealed by his blood in types and figures; and at his death in his flesh it was fully sealed and ratified by his blood itself *actually*, and indeed shed for our sins and in this respect it may be fitly called a *testament*. Because as a testament is not in force until the testator is dead, and where a testament is, there the death of the testator must come between to ratify it. So it is with the Covenant of Grace, and the promises in it made to us. Christ has performed and purchased all things necessary for us and freely gives to us himself, his righteousness, and all his treasures, as a man gives his lands and goods in his last will, but they cannot be in force to bring us to heaven, until his death comes between as a satisfaction for sin also. It is as necessary that justice should be satisfied for sin by his death, as righteousness of life performed, and salvation purchased by him for us. Secondly, as a man seals his testament when he sees or imagines that his death is at hand. So Christ at his last supper, by instituting the sacrament of his body and blood, and by the outward signs and seals in it contained, sealed to his church the Covenant of Grace. This is respect of Christ the Mediator, God and man, the Covenant of Grace, and the writings, Old and New, in which it is contained, are called *testaments*. But in respect of God the Father, and in respect of God, considered simply, or as the Maker of the covenant with man, and party between whom and man the covenant is made; the covenant and the writing, Old and New, in which it is comprehended, can in no case be called a testament, because a testament is of no force *without* the testator's death. But God the Father never died, nor can die, neither God simply considered, nor God the Maker of the covenant with man, and the other party in it which is opposed to man. Only Christ died as he was Mediator, God and man, and as he was made a partner with man, and stood on his side in the covenant, and as he is the testator, and free giver of his word in the Old and New Testament, and of his graces and gifts in it promised; so they are called testaments in this way, and in no other respect at all.

From the word *testament* expounded in this way we may easily collect and gather what is the nature of the testament, and both the agreement, and the true and main difference between the Old and New Testament, and the writing contained in both.

First, we see that they both agree in this, that they are the writings and instruments of one and the same Christ, and his last will, in which and by which he gives himself to his church with all his righteousness and obedience, and all the blessings which on this depend. They are both sealed by his blood and ratified by his death. This is manifest by the exposition of the word before laid down, in which is shown, that both the old and new writings of the covenant are called by the name *Testaments*, only in respect of Christ the Mediator, and as they are sealed by his blood, and ratified by his death. He is the Testator in them as he is Mediator. If either of them are not sealed, ratified and proceed from him as Mediator, it is no testament at all. We cannot call it a testament. That is to say that Christ is the Testator, and his death comes between to make it in force for us. And to say that he is not the Testator, or that it is not ratified by this death is to say, it is no testament. But all Christians grant that both the old and new writings of the covenant are *Testaments*. Therefore, it is manifest even by their names that Christ is Testator in both, that the legacies given are his gifts, even himself and all his treasures, and inheritance, that his blood heals, and his death ratifies both, and so in *substance* they agree, being of one Christ of the same things. Both are confirmed by one death, so they must necessarily be one, and confirm one another, and run one way. If they go various ways, they must necessarily destroy one another. If they do not destroy one another, it is plain. They both go one way, and confirm and illustrate each the other, which we evidently see. The difference then between them, is only in circumstance, and in quality, not in *substance*.

First, the Old Testament bequeathed to the fathers, righteousness of life, expiation of sin, adoption of sons, and eternal salvation, and happiness in and through Christ the Mediator promised, being not yet come in the flesh, but only seen a far off, and apprehended by faith, as the apostle shows, (Heb. 11). But the New Testament gives and bequeaths all these to us in and through Christ, being already come in the flesh, and having actually performed all things for us.

Secondly, the Old Testament was more dark and obscure, nor opened but to a few, until the Testator's death, and did not give birth to ordinarily so much knowledge and faith as the new does, and therefore it was a weaker means of grace, and converted but a few to Christ. But the New is so plain, that it may give birth to knowledge in children, and therefore by it the Spirit works more powerfully.

Thirdly, the Old Testament was sealed and ratified typically by the blood and death of Christ, and by types of them to come. The New is ratified by his death in very deed, and in itself, and to us it is sealed in the sacraments of the Lord's Supper by tokens and remembrances of his death already past and fulfilled.

Fourthly, the Old Testament, Christ the *Eternal Word* in his Godhead spoke to the fathers, and published by *Moses* and the prophets. But the New Testament he published by himself, immediately as he was God incarnate, and appeared in our nature, and by his apostles and evangelists, taught by his own mouth, as appears, (Heb. 1:2).

Fifthly, the Old Testament, in respect of the outward form and manner of sealing and signifying was temporary, and changeable, and therefore the types are ceased, and only the substance remains firm. But the New is unchangeable; and the seals of it are commemorative, and shall show the Lord's death until his coming again.

CHAPTER 3:
A TWO-FOLD USE

The doctrine of the former chapter is applied by way of use, to confute five differences which the schoolmen have made, and three differences which the Jesuits have added to them, between the Old and New Testament, and their vanity is discovered by this, and a two-fold use is moreover shown.

These and such like differences, the former exposition of the word *testament* may easily admit. For both the Old and the New may be testaments of Christ, that is, conveyances, and things bequeathed of *all* his graces and blessings, and may both be ratified by his death, and yet differ in these and such like respects. But as for diverse other differences which many learned men have set down, they are utterly overthrown by the exposition of the word *testament*, and by the true agreement which from there I have before gathered.

This therefore shall be the first use which I will make of these instructions, even to overthrow some other differences which the schoolmen have devised between the Old and New Testament. One is, that the Old Testament is *temporary and mutable*; the New *eternal and unchangeable*. This cannot stand, for if the Old Testament is a testament, it must necessarily be the testament of *Christ the Mediator* and if it was ever in force, it was *ratified* by the death of him the Testator (as is proved before). But if it was made in force by the death of Christ, how can it be *changeable*, surely in no way, except Christ's death is made *void* and of *no force*. Therefore the truth is, that though the Old Testament is in *quality* and *circumstance* changeable, and be changed in respect of the outward form and manner of sealing it to men, and where before it was dark and obscure, it has now become *bright and clear* by the coming of Christ, and the rising up of the Son of Righteousness, and by the fulfilling of the promises, and the doctrine of the Gospel in the New Testament. Yet it is not *changed* in substance, it does not lose the essence and being of a *testament*, but is Christ's instrument by which he gives and bequeaths all his treasures and benefits to us, as well as by the New. Yes, it is all *one* with the New in *substance*; it is the New folded up; and the New is the Old *opened* and *unfolded*. Those legacies which Christ gave to the fathers by the Old, are not made void, but are rather perfected by the New. And that which the Old gave by promise, the New gives by *actual performance in time*. The types which are in themselves abolished, stand firm forever in the things by them *signified*, which are their substance; and therefore the ceremonies of the Old Testament, are truly called "ordinances of eternity," (Exod. 12:14) and in diverse other places.

So we see the vanity of this first difference. Another difference which they make is that the New Testament was sealed with the blood of Christ, the Old with the blood of bullocks, goats, and other sacrifices. This also cannot stand with the former doctrine; for if the Old Testament is Christ's testament, and has been in force at any time; it was in force by virtue of Christ's death coming between (for otherwise no testament is in force, but by the death of the testator). And so it is *sealed* by Christ's blood. Now it is manifest by the former doctrine, that it is the testament of Christ and has been in force to the fathers (as all true Christians confess) and therefore it was sealed, not by the blood of bullocks only, but also by Christ's blood, and so this difference is not true. But because the words of the apostle seem to justify it, (Heb. 9) let me show how far it may be admitted, and in which it is faulty.

First, it is certain that the Old Testament was *outwardly sealed* at the first, and so long as it stood alone in force by the blood of bullocks and other sacrifices only. But it was in force *inwardly* by the blood of Christ alone, which was signified and represented in the blood of sacrifices. And at length when Christ came, and by the plain doctrine of the

Gospel had explained it, then it was together with the New, sealed *outwardly* by Christ's blood shed on the cross and his death on the cross. But the New was at the first outwardly sealed by the blood of Christ, and is now ever since daily to us outwardly sealed by the sacraments, and inwardly by Christ's blood in it signified. But to say that the Old Testament was not at all, nor at any time sealed with Christ's blood, but only by the blood of bullocks and sacrifices, and that the New Testament only was sealed with Christ's blood, is to make a *false* difference. For verily the Old Testament being nothing else but the New folded up, and the New the Old opened to all; the sealing of the New by Christ's blood, was the sealing of the Old also. Yes, as our sacraments, and the outward signs consecrated to signify of the Law and the Old Testament true signs, consecrated to signify Christ's death to come; and as our seal the New Testament, so did they seal the Old. As with our right outward sealing, there goes the inward sealing of Christ's blood; so also with those outward seals rightly understood, and used. And therefore as it is absurd to say that the New Testament is sealed *only* by bread and wine, and water, when we administer and receive the sacraments, because we do not use other outward signs; so it is absurd to say of their sacrifices, that in them there is not sealing, but by blood of beasts sacrificed; and so we see the vanity of this difference also.

The third difference which the schoolmen make, and which only the *papists* do hold, is, that the Old Testament did only promise eternal blessings, and the eternal inheritance, and foreshow them in types, as in the blood sacrifices through Christ's blood, in the Promised Land, the inheritance of heaven, and such like, but it did not give the blessings to them until Christ the Testator was *dead*. But the New Testament promises, and also gives and exhibits the things promised. This difference is very *false and impious*, and is easily confuted by the former doctrine, and by the whole Scriptures. For that which only promises, and is not given, is *not a testament*, it is never *in force*, neither *ratified* at all, for being in force by the testator's death, must necessarily *give* as well as *promise*. If the testator's death never comes between, then it is not a testament. But the Old is a testament, and was in force, and gave, and gives grace, as well as promises it.

This the whole Scriptures show; for the legacies promised and given in Christ's will, are himself, with all his benefits which accompany him. Let us consider this in the following points.

First, his conception and birth, most holy without spot, to sanctify our conception in sin, and our unclean birth.

Secondly, his perfect righteousness of life, to make believers righteous.

Thirdly, his death and sufferings, to ransom them from eternal death, and hell, by satisfying for their sins.

Fourthly, his Spirit, with all saving graces, as faith, and such like, by which they come to have communion with him of his Sonship, inheritance, righteousness, and right to all blessings, temporal, and spiritual.

Now though Christ was only promised in the Old Testament, that he should *come*, and *obey*, and *suffer* for man's redemption; but was not *actually* exhibited, nor obeyed and suffered until the days of the New Testament, yet his manhood, birth, obedience and death, were *then* as effectual to save the faithful, as they are now. And in that respect he is called *the Lamb slain from the beginning of the world*. Also by the words of promise in the Old Testament, Christ communicated and gave his Spirit to *Adam, Noah, Abraham, David,* and all the faithful in the Old Testament, which Spirit worked in them faith and perfect communion with Christ, of his person so far as to make them sons and heirs of God, of his death for remission of their sins; of his righteousness for their justification, and of all saving graces needful to salvation. This appears by *Enoch's* translation into glory, that he might not see death, and by *Elijah's* taking up into heaven by virtue of

Christ's resurrection and ascension, who is the first fruits from the beginning. Also by that which is said of *Abraham*, that he *by believing* came to be counted righteous. And by that which *David* says to himself, "That God is his portion," (Psalm 16:5) and with him he had all things to make him blessed.

Therefore this difference is a blasphemous and wicked fiction, excluding the church of the Old Testament from heaven, and all fruition of Christ's benefits, and from all saving graces, as regeneration, remission of sins, justification, and redemption, which are the blessings promised and given in the Old Testament.

The fourth difference is, that the New Testament is the end of the Old, and the Old is but a means to obtain the New, which is the idea of the Jesuits. This is confuted, first by the doctrine before; for they which are both in substance, one, and the same testament, cannot the one be the end of the other. But so are these two, as I have before showed. And it is manifested most by the agreement between them, that as the Old *confirms* the New, and serves to move men to receive it. So the New being embraced, serves to give light to the Old, that men may see into the true meaning of it, and rightly understand it, and so here is no difference, in this respect they are both alike.

Secondly, they Scripture is plain, (even in the places which they cite to prove this difference, in other words, Rom. 10:4 and Gal. 3:24), and teaches plainly that Christ is the end of both, and both serve jointly for this one and common end, to bring men to Christ, and to perfect communion with him. Therefore the New is no otherwise the end of the Old, than the Old is the end of the New, and so this difference is false and erroneous.

This fifth difference is, that the Old Testament was given only to the natural Israelites; the New to the entire world. This is here by the former doctrine proved false. For if the Old Testament is the will of Christ, as Mediator, who gave himself for all the nations of the world, and is one in *substance* with the New, and gives the same legacies, as is before showed, surely they were both given to all nations, even the Old as well as the New. What else what shall we say of *Job*, and the godly and faithful of his country and age, mentioned in his book, who had the promises sealed with bloody sacrifices, and yet were not of the nation of Israel? Only here is the difference; the natural Israelites had the keeping of the Old Testament, and the oracles of God committed to them *for a time*, in other words, from Mosestill Christ: And yet even then it was lawful for them to teach the word, and make known the promises to strangers of all nations, and to convert them, and to receive them into the church. And many were converted, and joined themselves to the God of Israel. "Also the sons of the stranger, that join themselves to the LORD, to serve him, and to love the name of the LORD, to be his servants, every one that keepeth the sabbath from polluting it, and taketh hold of my covenant," (Isa. 56:6). As *Rahab* of Jericho, a Canaanitess, *Ruth* of Moah, *Ebed-melech* of Ethiopia, and diverse others. But the New Testament is committed to no special *people*, but published to the entire world and among all nations. So now is the Old also, and serves ever since Christ for the instruction of all nations of the Gentiles. Therefore this difference is *false*. To these the Jesuits[1] have added three differences more, which are so gross, and abominable, that they need no confutation. One is that the New Testament went before the Old, because the promises of Christ went before the giving of the Law, 430 years. Here they show much ignorance; for the Old Testament consists of the promises, as well as of the Law, and the promises are the chief things in it; so that the promises and it go together, and they are no more before it, then it is before itself. If they will perversely by the Old Testament understand only the Law of

---

[1] The arguments which the Jesuits put forth, as refuted clearly by Walker, seem characteristic of Baptist theology, which remain dispensational. It is uncanny how the Jesuits reflect the same ideas that modern dispensationalists refer to or attempt to defend today with little or no recourse from Reformed Christians.

Moses, having no respect to the promise of Christ, they are in a gross error. For that can in no way be called the testament of Christ, for it has nothing to do with the Mediator, he does not bequeath anything to his church in that way.

Another difference is, that the Old Testament, did not quicken any nor give spiritual blessings, but only temporary. But the New Testament gives life and spiritual blessings, even the kingdom of heaven. The Old gave but the *shadow*, the New gives the *substance*, the Old the shell, the New the kernel. This is also a mistaking of the Old Testament for the bare letter of the Law, without respect to Christ. Otherwise their speech is most abominable. For God by the promises in the Old Testament quickened many, and brought them to Christ, and to all grace and blessedness in him, as we see in *Abraham*, *David*, and the holy prophets. So that if by the Old Testament they understand rightly all the writing of *Moses* and the prophets before Christ, they are in a blasphemous *error*. If only they mean by the Old Testament, the Law without any promises of Christ, then it is no testament, and so they err grossly to call it so.

The last difference is that the New Testament makes men sons, and brings them also to the state of sons. But the Old makes no one *sons*, except by virtue of the New, neither does it bring anyone to the state of sons, but all under it lived as children under bondage, as the apostle speaks, (Gal. 4). This is also proved to be *false* by the former doctrine; for whoever is in Christ *are* sons, and whoever has the Spirit of adoption, *are* sons of God, and *in* the state of sons. Now the Old Testament brings all the faithful fathers to Christ, and to true fellowship and communion with him, otherwise none of them could have been saved. Neither could it have been a testament, one in substance with the New (Acts 4:12). Yes, the Scripture testifies plainly, that the faithful under the Old Testament were sons of God, for they are brought in this way speaking to God, "Doubtless thou art our Father, though Abraham be ignorant of us, and Israel acknowledge us not. Thou, O Lord, art our Father, and our Redeemer, thy name is from everlasting," (Isa. 63:16). And Isa. 64:8, and "I am a Father to Israel (*God says*) and Ephraim is my first born," (Jer. 31:9). And yet all these had no other means to bring them in this way near to God but by the Old Testament. Therefore we see there is no such difference between the Old and the New Testament, as many would have us to believe, only they differ in some circumstances, and in quality, as in plainness of revelation, and such like before named; and yet now the difference is not so great, when the Old is laid open and expounded by the New, and daily more and more explained to us. And so much for the first use.

Secondly, this truth well considered is of special use to make us esteem and reverence the Old Testament as well as the New, and so to respect and honor the New, that in the meantime we do not neglect or lightly esteem the Old Testament. Let blasphemous heretics say what they will, let some of them call it a *killing letter*, and the *ministry of death*, and make the prince of darkness the author of it, and others *blaspheme* it, as a covenant only of carnal and earthly promises. Yet let all true Christians honor and embrace it as the word of the most High, holy, and only true God, and the testament of Christ sealed with his blood, and ratified by his death, in which the fathers found salvation, and eternal life, as our Savior shows, "Search the scriptures; for in them ye think ye have eternal life: and they are they which testify of me," (John 5:39).

Thirdly, this doctrine serves to reach and direct us in the right way both of understanding and expounding the obscure prophecies of the Old Testament, and confirming, by the Old, the most doubtful things rehearsed in the New; for the prophets of old spoke of Christ, and of all things which are recorded in the Gospel concerning his death, and sufferings for our redemption. And if any should doubt of the things written in the Gospel, concerning the ignominious death and sufferings of Christ, as being too base for the Son of God to suffer; the Old Testament will confirm all, and will show that God himself from the beginning foretold Christ's death, when he said, "that the serpent should bruise his heel," (Gen. 3:15); and by the slaughter and bloody sacrifices of beasts, in types foreshowed the same.

The prophets also from *Moses*, in all the Scriptures, foretold whatever Christ did or suffered in the flesh for man's redemption; as our Savior showed to the two disciples in the way to Emmaus (Luke 24). And as the New Testament is confirmed by the Old; so the Old receives clear light from the New, and that which in it was more obscurely foretold, is by the fulfilling of it in the New, made more clear and evident. Therefore let us receive them both as *one and the same* Testament in *substance*, and that of one and the *same* Christ. If we make them both look one way, and in expounding them make Christ the matter and subject of both, we shall not err, nor be deceived, but in both together we shall see Christ most fully revealed, so far as is needful for us to know him, and the true way to salvation, in him our Savior and Redeemer.

CHAPTER 4:
COVENANT

What the word covenant signifies, what is the nature of a covenant in general.

The second thing which needs to be considered, is the covenant between God and man. Here we are to show what the word *covenant* signifies, what is the nature of a covenant, and the agreement and difference between the Old and New Covenant. The word *covenant*, in our English tongue, signifies, as we all know, *a mutual promise*, but *gain and obligation between two parties*, and so likewise the Hebrew word בְּרִית (*beriyth*) and the Greek word διαθήκη (*diatheke*) signify most commonly. But the derivation of the Hebrew word, and of the Greek, is of *special* use, to show the *nature* of the covenant which they principally signify, and what special things are required in it. I will therefore first insist upon it a little. Secondly, I will show the several sorts of covenants which the words signify, and will briefly describe all the covenants between God and men. Thirdly, out of the several descriptions I will gather the agreement and difference between the Old and the New

Covenant. And lastly, I will make some use and application of these considerations to ourselves.

First the derivation of the words, if it is rightly considered, may give the substance of the word *Berith*, which is derived from *Bara*, which means to purify, and to purge out dross, chaff, and all uncleanness, and to choose one, and separate the pure from the impure, the gold and silver from the dross, and the pure wheat from the chaff. The reasons of this derivation, are two. One, because God, in making the covenant of *natural life*, chose out man especially with whom he would make the covenant. And in the Covenant of Grace he chooses out the multitude of the elect, even his church and faithful people, whom he separated by predestination, and election, from all eternity, to be an holy people to himself in Christ. The other reason is, because in a true and lawful covenant both parties must be of pure hearts, free from all deceit and sophistry, and must deal faithfully, and be plain and sincere in every point and article.

Others derive the word *Berith* of *Bera*, which signifies *election*. God made the first Covenant of Grace, and sealed it by sacrifices of beasts, slain, divided, and cut asunder, and the *choice* fat and other parts offered upon the altars and in making of great and solemn covenants, men in old time were accustomed to kill and cut asunder sacrifices beasts, and to pass between the parts divided for a solemn testimony (Gen. 15:17; Jer. 34:18). Others derive the word *Berith* from ברה *Barah* which signifies to eat and refresh oneself with meat, in which there is some reason. Because the old covenant of God, made with man in the creation, was a covenant in which the condition or law was about *eating*. Man should eat of all trees and fruits, except of the Tree of Knowledge of Good and Evil. And in the solemn making and sealing of the Covenant of Grace in Christ the blessed seed, the public ceremony was slaying and sacrificing of beasts, and eating some part of them, after the fat and choice parts were offered up and burnt of the altar. For God by virtue of that covenant gave men leave to eat the flesh of beasts, which he might not do in the state of innocency, being limited to fruits of trees, and herbs bearing seed, for his meat (Gen. 1:29). So also in solemn covenants between men, the parties were "accustomed to eat together," (Gen. 31:46).

To these, two other derivations may be added; one, that *Berith* may be derived of ברא (*bara'*) which signifies to create, of which there is good reason; in other words, because the first state of creation was confirmed by the *covenant* which God made with man, and all creatures were to be upheld by means of observing of the Law and condition of the covenant.

And the covenant being broken by man, the world made subject to rules is upheld; yes, and as it was created anew by the Covenant of Grace in Christ.

The other derivation is of the Hebrew word בָּרִיא (*bariy'*) which signifies *fat*. In the Covenant of Grace, God promises to man the *fat* of heaven, and of the earth, that is, the most excellent blessings which heaven and earth can afford. And man offers up to God the *fat* of his soul, and of all his good, that is, the most precious things which he has, besides the sweet and most excellent and precious sacrifice which Christ offers up for him to God.

These are the diverse derivations of the *Berith*, which I have observed out of the writings of the learned, to which I have added these two last.

And because this word well agrees with the sound and signification of all the words of which it is derived by several learned men, so that if we should make choice of any one derivation we might seem to reject and despise others which stand with good reason, I hold it the safest and surest way to account of this word, as of a *special* word invented and given by the Spirit of God himself, who sees and knows all circumstance of everything at once, and that it is purposely framed out of all the words before named. It includes in it the sum of them all, being as it were; the *quintessence* of them all distilled together into one perfect sense. And however it may seem strange to some, at the first blush, that one word should be derived of many, and receive a mixed signification from them all; yet if they consider it more, they shall see good reason for it, and shall find that it is not a rare thing in holy Scripture for one word to signify in one place diverse things, and one word to be derived of many, and to borrow the several significations of them all.

The proper name of the prophet *Samuel*, is derived of four Hebrew words, the first *Shaal*, which signifies to ask; the second *Hu*, which signifies him; the third *Min*, which signifies of; the fourth *El*, which signifies God. And it is said that his mother called him *Samuel*, that is, one asked of God, because she said, "I asked him of the Lord," (1 Sam. 1:20). So the prophet *Isaiah* called his son by God's appointment *Shearjashub* (Isa. 7:3), which is derived from several words which signify, a remnant shall return. And the prophet *Jeremiah*, by inspiration of God's Spirit, told *Pashur* the persecuting priest, that his name should be *Magormissabib* (Jer. 20:3), terror round about, or on every side, because the Lord would make him a terror to himself. Now if one name may by the testimony of God's Spirit be derived of diverse words, and borrow a mixed sense from them all, as *Samuel*, which is derived or compounded of four words, and holds the signification of them all, though it includes but one letter of some of them, much more may we think that the word *Berith* is derived of all the words before named, and includes in it the sense and signification of them all, as well as it includes a syllable at least of every one of them. This is one strong and invincible reason. Secondly, we have good reasons of every derivation, as I have already shown. Thirdly, the deriving of the word, from all, and not from one only, reconciles in one, all the several opinions of the learned, and justifies their several derivations, without rejecting, or offering any wrong, or disgrace to any. Fourthly, the Greek word διαθήκη (*diatheke*), by which the Septuagint in their Greek translation expresses the Hebrew word *Berith* is derived; for it signifies to set things in order and frame, to appoint orders, and make laws, to pacify and make satisfaction, and to dispose things by one's last will and testament. Now to compose and set things in frame, is to uphold the creation; to walk by orders and laws made and appointed, is to walk by rules, and to live and to deal plainly, and faithfully, without deceit. To pacify and make satisfaction includes sacrifices and sin offerings. To dispose by will and testament, implies choice of persons and gifts; for men do by will give their best and most choice goods to their most dear and most choice friends. So the Greek, which the apostles use in the New, and the Septuagint in the Old Testament to signify a covenant, to express the Hebrew word *Berith*, which is used in the Law and the Prophets, confirms our derivation of it from all the words before named. And this derivation of the Hebrew and Greek names of a *covenant* being in this way laid down and confirmed by these reasons, is of great *use:*

First, to show to us the full signification of the word *covenant*, and what the nature of a covenant is in general.

Secondly, to justify the diverse acceptations of the word, and to show the nature of every word in particular; and so to make way for the knowledge of the agreement, and difference between the Old and New Covenant.

First, there we see that this word signifies all covenants in general, both God's covenant with men, and also the covenant which men make among themselves. For there is nothing in any true covenant, which is not comprised in the signification of this word, being expounded according to the former derivations.

Here also we see what is the nature of a covenant in general, and what things are there to it required.

First, every true covenant presupposes a division, or separation.

Secondly, it comprehends in it a mutual promising, and binding between two distinct parties.

Thirdly, there must be faithful dealing, without fraud, or dissembling, on both sides.

Fourthly, this must be between choice persons.

Fifthly, it must be about choice matters, and on choice conditions, agreed on by both.

Sixthly, it must tend to the well-ordering and composing of things between them. All these are manifest by the significance of the words from which *Berith* is derived. But I do not hold it so needful to stand on the nature of a covenant in general. I therefore come with speed to the diverse acceptations of the word, and to the description of every special, and particular covenant, which is needful to be known of us.

CHAPTER 5:
TYPES OF COVENANTS

The several kinds of covenants between God and men. The Covenant of Nature is described. The Covenant of Grace is unfolded, and the blessings in it promised are rehearsed. That this covenant is a covenant of free grace is plainly proved. The division of it into the Old and New Covenant.

First, the Hebrew word *Berith*, (as also the names of covenant, in the Greek, and English tongue) signifies a covenant between God and man.

Secondly, it signifies the covenants of men among themselves, (Gen. 21:27). It signifies the covenant between *Abraham* and *Abimelech*, and the covenant between *Jacob* and *Laban*, (Gen. 31:44). But here I have little to do with covenants between men. The covenant which I am to insist on, is between God and men.

First, the covenant of natural life and blessings, which God made with man in the creation.

Secondly, the *Covenant of Grace*, which God made with man in Christ, after man's fall. In the *Covenant of Nature*, the parties were, God the Creator, and man the creature, made after God's image and likeness, and so not contrary to God, nor at enmity with him, but like to God, though far different, and inferior to God, in nature and substance. The promises on God's part were these, that heaven and earth and all creatures should continue in their natural course and order, in which God had created and placed them, serving always for man's use, and that man should have their benefit, and lordship, and should live happily, and never see death. The condition on man's part was *obedience* to God's law, and *subjection* to God his Creator in *all things*; and this he was to express by obeying God's voice in *everything* which he had already, or should at *any time command*, more especially in abstaining from the Tree of Good and Evil. The sign and seal which God gave to man, for the confirmation of the covenant, was the *Tree of Life*, which was to man a *sacrament*, and *pledge* of eternal life on earth, and of all blessings needful to keep man in life. The receiving of this seal, was man's *eating* of the Tree of Knowledge. The end of this covenant, was the upholding of the creation, and of all the creatures in their pure natural estate, for the comfort of man continually.

This was the first covenant which God made with man, and this is called by the name *Berith*, where God says, "If you can break my covenant of the day and night, and that there shall not be day and night in their season, then may also my covenant with *David* be broken," (Jer. 33:20-21).

In those words he speaks plainly of the promise in the creation, "That day and night should keep their course, and the sun, moon, and stars, and all creatures should serve for man's use," (Gen. 1:14-16) This though man *did* break on his part, yet God, being immutable, could *not* break it, neither did he suffer his promise to fade; but, by virtue of *Christ* promised to man in the New Covenant he does in some good measure continue it, so long as mankind has a being on earth.

The Covenant of Grace, is that which God made with man *after* his fall, in which of his own free grace and mercy, he promises to mankind a blessed seed of the woman, which by bruising the serpent's head, that is, destroying the power and works of the devil, should redeem mankind, and restore all that believe in the blessed seed Christ, to a more happy and blessed estate, then that which was lost. In this covenant the parties were God Almighty offended by man's sin, and provoked to just wrath; and man by his willful transgression now became a rebel and enemy against God, and deserving eternal death, so that here is great contrariety, separation, opposition, and ease of enmity between the two parties, and between them there was no possibility of peace and reconciliation, without a fit and all sufficient Mediator necessarily coming between.

The things which God promises in the covenant, and for his part performs, are admirable, far surpassing man's reason.

The first, is the all-sufficient Mediator Christ, his own eternal Son, whom God promised immediately after man's fall, and who did then begin; actually, to mediate for man; and undertook to become man, and by a full satisfaction made in man's nature; to God's infinite justice, and just Law, and a perfect and full ransom paid for man's redemption to purchase pardon of all man's sins; to justice, and make him righteous, and to reconcile him to God.

The second, is the Spirit to be given to man, and shed on him through Christ the Mediator, (Gal. 3:14; Titus 3:6).

The third, is spiritual life, derived from Christ, and wrought in man by his quickening Spirit, together with all graces and blessings belonging to it.

The fourth, is union, and communion with Christ of all his benefits, as of his Sonship, to make all regenerate men sons of God, and heirs of eternal life, glory, and all blessings, of his satisfaction and sufferings for remission of all their sins; of his righteousness for justification.

The fifth, is a true right to the natural life which *Adam* lost, to the creatures made for man's use, and to all earthly blessings which are given him to possess and enjoy in this life.

The sixth, is sanctification and holiness, by which man is fitted to see and enjoy God, (Matt. 5:8; Heb. 12:14).

The last, which is the end of all, is the eternal life of glory, in the fruition of God in heaven.

In this covenant there is not any condition or law to be performed on man's part by man himself, as in the first old covenant, of Nature; and therefore it is called the free Covenant of Grace, and not of works. The perfect obedience, righteousness, and satisfaction of Christ, which he performed to the whole Law, for man, in man's nature, though it stands in the place of every man's perfect obedience to God's Law in his own person, and his subjection to the whole revealed will of God, which was the condition of the old Covenant of Works, and when man is partaker of it by communion with Christ, he is more perfectly justified, and made worthy of life eternal, than man in the state of nature could have been by his own perfect obedience, and personal righteousness performed in his own person; Yet it cannot so properly be called, a condition of the New Covenant of Grace which God has made with mankind (because God does not impose it as a condition to be performed by every man in his own person) but is one of the blessings promised in the New Covenant. So likewise, the gifts, graces, and works, and fruit of the Spirit, which are required to be in man, to make him an actual partaker of Christ, and of life and salvation in him, whether they are outward, as the word preached and heard, the sacraments given and received, and the like; or inward, as faith, by which Christ is received, and applied; repentance, love, hope, and other saving graces; they are all free gifts of God, he gives them to us, and by his Spirit works in us both to will and to do, and without his grace continually assisting us according to his promise, we cannot perform anything which is mentioned in the Gospel, as a conditional means of life and salvation in Christ. And therefore this covenant is *fadus gratuitnim,* a most *free* Covenant of Grace, in which no condition is propounded to man, to be performed by any power of his own, for the obtaining of life. By God of his own free grace promises all blessings, and for *his own sake* gives them; and also all power to receive and enjoy them. And the end and use of the covenant, is not any gain which God seeketh to himself, nor any good which he can receive from man, or any creature, but only the making of man perfectly blessed in the fruition of himself and all his goodness, and so gathering to himself all things in Christ. This covenant is that which is called *the Covenant of Peace,* and is most highly extolled, and commended in all the Scriptures, both of the Old and New Testament. And however the substance of this covenant has been always one and the same from the beginning, even from the seventh day of the world; in which God first promised Christ the blessed seed; and so shall be forever, yet because the circumstances are diverse, and the manner of revealing the promise, and of sealing it, is far different in the Old, and New Testament; on this it comes to pass, that the Spirit of God distinguishes it into the Old and New Covenant; and as it was revealed, and sealed to the fathers under the Law, calls it the Old Covenant; and as it now revealed and sealed under the Gospel, calls it the New Covenant (Jer. 31:31; 2 Cor. 3:6). And both these are called by the name *berith* in the Hebrew, and by the name of *diathake* in the Greek text.

CHAPTER 6:
THE COVENANT OF GRACE

The Covenant of Grace first made with Adam after his fall. The liberty by it given to man proves that we gain more by Christ then we lost in Adam. Of the renewing of it with Noah. The forces of renewing it with Abraham, and revealing it more plainly by seven things. Of the renewing of it with Israel and Mount Sinai and by Moses. That it is called the Old Covenant in respect of the New Covenant in the Gospel. That it is mixed of the Covenant of Works and of the Covenant of Grace. The reasons why God is making it did renew the Covenant of Works, and mingle it with the Covenant of Grace made with man in Christ after his fall.

In the Old Testament, the Lord first made this covenant with *Adam*, but in very dark, obscure, and general terms, and in types and figures, even sacrifices which were seals of it to him and his posterity. The words of the covenant were these, "That the seed of the woman should break the serpent's head, and the serpent should bruise his heel," (Gen. 3:15), that is, "Christ made man of the seed of woman," (Rom. 1:3); and being by the old serpent, the devil, and by the generation of vipers persecuted, and put to an ignominious death, should dissolve the works of the devil, and destroy sin, by satisfying for it to the full. The sacrifices which God added to this promise, further to illustrate and confirm it, were clean and fat-fed beasts, which the Lord commanded them to consecrate, slay and to offer up to him by burning and consuming part of it; and the rest they themselves who were his priests and sacrificers ate. That the Lord taught *Adam* to sacrifice appears by the practice of *Cain* and *Abel*, and by their offerings which they brought to God, being undoubtedly taught by their father, (Gen. 4). Yes, it may be gathered from the coats of skins which God made, and therewith clothed our first parents, (Gen. 3:21). These skins could be no other, but of beasts slain and offered in sacrifice. For before *Adam's* fall, beasts were not subject to mortality, nor slain; the slaughter, and killing of beasts, and man's eating of their flesh, came in by sin, and after man's fall. In innocency man's meat was fruit of trees, and herbs bearing seed, (Gen. 1).

The first right which God gave to man to eat flesh, was after the promise, and after that beasts were consecrated to be sacrificed as types of Christ, and of his death. Now these sacrifices of beasts did show the nature of the covenant, and the manner of man's reconciliation; choosing of clean and harmless beasts, showed that Christ should be pure and holy in himself; like a lamb without spot. The consecration of them showed that Christ should in his conception be sacrificed, and take our nature, and our sins upon him; that he might be our Redeemer, and our Sacrifice. The killing of the beasts, and the burning of the fat, and some parts of them, signified the manner of Christ's reconciling of us, and working our peace, even by his death; and passing through the fire of God's wrath. God's clothing of *Adam* and his wife with their skins, signified that man's sin and shame is covered with Christ's satisfaction, and the faithful are to be clothed with the robe of his righteousness.

The liberty which God gave man to eat flesh of beasts, which he might not before sacrifices were ordained, shows that we gain more by Christ, than we lost in *Adam*. This was the first making and revealing of the covenant.

Afterwards the Lord renewed this covenant with *Noah*, (Gen. 6:10), and further revealed it in another type, namely, the saving of *Noah* and his family in the ark, which was borne up by the flood of waters; which ark signified the church. The saving of them only who were in the ark showed that salvation is found only the church of Christ, and none can be saved, but they who by faith cleave to Christ, and are members of his body in the true church. The water bearing up the ark, and so saving it and them that were in it, signified that the church and faithful are saved by the washing of regeneration, (Titus 3:5). The baptism of the Spirit, and that laver of Christ's blood, which outward baptism signifies, (1 Peter 3:21).

Thirdly, the Lord renewed this covenant with *Abraham*, and did somewhat more plainly reveal it to him.

First, by promise, that in him all the families of the earth should be blessed, and the promised seed and Savior should come of him, (Gen. 12:3, 22:18).

Secondly, by showing the way to life and happiness, even justification by faith, apprehending Christ, and seeking righteousness for a shield, and for reward in him alone, (Gen. 15:16).

Thirdly, by oath, (Gen. 22:16).

Fourthly, by the promise of the land of Canaan to him, and to his seed, which was the type of the heavenly Canaan, and prefigured the country which is above, (Gen. 15:18).

Fifthly, by the seal of the Covenant of Grace, in other words, circumcision, which signified that God's faithful people must be circumcised in their hearts, and have the foreskin of fleshly lusts cut away by mortification of the Spirit, (Gen. 17).

Sixthly, the offering up of *Isaac*, the son of promise, on Mount Moriah, by God's appointment, prefigured and foreshowed, that by the offering up of Christ, the promised seed, in the same place, all nations should be saved, God's wrath pacified, and perfect obedience fulfilled.

Lastly, by the outward form, and ceremony of a solemn oath and covenant which passed between God and *Abraham*, (Gen. 15:17). For there we read, that the Lord commanded *Abraham* to take an heifer of three years old, a she goat of three years, and a ram of three years, and a turtle dove, and young pigeon, and he divided them in the midst, and laid each piece, one against another. And it came to pass, that when the sun went down, and it was dark, behold a smoking furnace, and a burning lamp, that passed between those pieces. Now this was the form of taking a solemn oath among the Chaldeans and the Hebrews, instituted by God himself, as appears in Jer. 34:18, where it is said, that when the children of Israel made a covenant to let their servants go free, they cut a calf in twain, and passed between the parts of it. This was the ceremony of an oath and covenant; and this God ordained, for he calls it there, his covenant. And on this it is, that in the Old Testament, the Hebrew word which is used for making of a covenant, is בְּרִית (*beriyth*), (which signifies, to *cut asunder*) as appears, (Deut. 5:2) and diverse other places, which showeth that covenants were solemnly made by sacrifices of beasts divided.

Now this dividing of the beasts in two parts, signified and teach two things.

First, that there was a division made between God and men, by sin.

Secondly, the division of the Covenant of Grace, into two parts, the Old and New Testament. The coming, and passing between signified.

First, that God and men needs be reconciled, and the covenant sealed and confirmed between them by a Mediator.

Secondly, that Christ the Mediator was to come in the middle of years, between the time of the Old, and the time of the New Testament, to knit and link both in one, and to confirm both. But in that God came between the parts, like a smoking furnace, and a burning lamp, to confirm the covenant and to seal it to *Abraham* at that time this signified.

First, that Christ the Mediator, coming between God and men, should be God clouded in our frail nature which is but like a vapor and smoke; that he should pass through the furnace of afflictions; and yet in his life should be a burning and shining lamp, pure and perfection righteousness and holiness.

Secondly, that the Lord in those times revealed himself and his Son more obscurely, like a smoking furnace in smoke and clouds, arid like a burning lamp, which is but dim in comparison of the light of Christ the Son of Righteousness, risen up in the Gospel, and the brightness of God's glory shining in the face of Jesus Christ.

Besides these we read of diverse other renewings, and explanation of this covenant; as that with *David*, recorded, (Psalm 89:3, 28, 34) *verifies*; where the Lord promised that Christ should come of the seed of *David*, and should be a King forever, (Psalm 89:4). And many promises of special blessings which God of old promised, are called *covenants*. But the special and principal covenant which is promised called the Old, and is distinguished from the New Covenant of the Gospel, is God's making and renewing of the covenant with Israel, partly by his own mouth, and partly by the ministry of *Moses* on Mount Horeb, which is mentioned in Exodus 19:20. For that covenant is a *mixed covenant*, partly of the Covenant of Works, which is the Old Covenant, partly of the Covenant of Grace, which was made after the fall.

First, God sent *Moses* to the people to ask whether they would obey the Lord's voice, and keep all his Commandments, that they might by them live and be blessed. They answered all together, and said, "All that the Lord hath spoken we will do," (Exod. 19:8). On this the Lord came down on Mount Sinai, in fire and smoke and with terrible thunders and lightnings, and the sound of a trumpet, and spoke to them the words of the Law immediately with his own mouth, promising life to them that kept it, and threatening death to those who would break it.

Now this was but a *repeating*, and *renewing* of the first Covenant of Works, to be performed by every man in his own person, for the obtaining of life. In this therefore there was no mediator between God and the people.

The reasons why the Lord began this way with Israel, and first renewed the Old Covenant, were diverse.

The first, was their pride, presumption, and hardness of heart; they presumed that they could do all that the Lord would command them, and therefore he gave them his Law to show them their duty; that they assaying to fulfill it, and finding their own insufficiency, might be humbled and brought down from vain confidence in their own works.

Here the Lord dealt with them as wise fathers deal with their foolish and vain boasting sons, who promises largely that they will do anything which their father will command them, and that by their merits they will bind their fathers to love them, and to give them the inheritance. In such a case, a wise father will put such a boasting son to the trial, and will put him to a task which he knows that he is unable to go through; not because he believes, or hopes that his sin can perform it (being through his own intemperance disabled) but for this end, to make him see his own folly and insufficiency. And so the Lord dealt with Israel.

Secondly, the Lord gave the Law, which is the rule of righteousness, and with all showed the punishment due to the transgressors of it; that it might be as the rod of a schoolmaster, to drive them to Christ, to learn the saving knowledge, and way of life in him, as the apostle speaks, (Gal. 3) and to make them out of fear renounce themselves, and seek mercy in him.

Thirdly, to reach them and us, that however it is impossible for us to be saved by the Law, by reason of our sinful flesh, and our corruption which hath utterly disable us, that we cannot obey it; yet the Law is still in force, and requires perfect righteousness; and without the righteousness of the Law fulfilled by Christ for us, we cannot be justified nor saved, according to the saying of the apostle, "Christ is the end of the Law for righteousness to everyone that believeth," (Rom. 10:4).

But when the people of Israel heard the Law, which was the *Covenant of Works* to be performed in their own persons, and that immediately from God himself, it is said that they were sore afraid, and being not able to abide the sight of God's glory, nor the sound of this voice, they cried out, "Why should we die?" (Deut. 5:25) and on this they began to desire a mediator, even *Moses*, saying "Go thou and hear the Lord, and speak thou to us," (Exod. 20:19; Deut. 5:25-27). This was some good beginning; the Law began to take effect, and to drive them towards a mediator. And therefore the Lord said, "They have well-spoken all that they have said," (Deut. 18:17) in other words, in desiring a mediator; and added with, "O that there were in them such an heart, that they would fear me, and keep my commandments always: that it might be well with them and their children," (Deut. 5:29). Which words show the will and mind of God, wishing after a sort their increase and continuance in this good mind and fear of him, and seeking to keep his commandment, in and by a mediator. On which he proceeds to deal with them by a Mediator, and to renew the covenant with them, by appointing diverse figures of Christ, as sacrifices, rites, ceremonies, the tabernacle, the ark of covenant, and the mercy seat; in all which, as in types, he revealed Christ, though obscurely, to them, and shown that sin was to be expiated and purged away by his death.

Afterward, also when they came in the land of Moab, he renewed the Covenant of Grace in more plain terms than he did on Mount Horeb; insomuch that by reason of the greater plainness, it is called *another* covenant, (Deut. 29:2). There he told them, that Christ should be their rock, (Deut. 32:4) and that the word, his Gospel, was among them.

Now because of the first part of this covenant, in other words, the Ten Commandments which God spoke first; and after gave them written in two tables, which are called by the name of *covenant*, (Deut. 4:13; 9:9) and indeed are the summary of the Old Covenant which God made with men in the creation.

This covenant, which God made with Israel is called the Old Covenant, and the covenant of the Law, and is opposed to the covenant of Gospel, that is, to the covenant as it is now revealed in the writings of the evangelists and apostles, and plainly preached and published over all the world.

So much for the *Old Covenant*.

CHAPTER 7:
THE COVENANT OF GRACE AND THE GOSPEL

Of the New Covenant of Grace, as it is made most plainly in the Gospel, and in the New Testament. The reasons why it is called the New Covenant.

The New Covenant which was foretold by the prophets, (Isa. 42:6; Jer. 31:31; Zach. 9:1); it is the covenant which God has newly made by the preaching of the Gospel in this New Testament. It is the *covenant of all happiness,* all blessings, and all salvation in Christ, plainly preached and revealed, sealed also and confirmed, not by blood of Christ in types and figures, but by the *very* blood itself bodily shed on the cross for our sins; and by the two plain sacraments of baptism, and the Lord's Supper. This is called וְכָרַתִּי *the New Covenant,* (Jer. 31:31), and καινὴ διαθήκη, (Luke 22:20), and καινῆς διαθήκης , (2 Cor. 3:6), κρείττονος διαθήκης, a better covenant, (Heb. 7:22). For in it the Lord reveals his promises so plainly and clearly, that all men may see and know the way of life. And in the covenant there is *nothing* expressed which was not implied and included in the general obscure promises made to *Adam*, and unto *Abraham*, and *David*, and the rest of the fathers in old time, as Jesus Christ is the perfect Savior, and Eternal Redeemer. God and man, with all his righteousness, obedience, and full satisfaction, and all his benefits, blessings, gifts, and graces, which serve to bring men to perfect blessedness and salvation; and which are fully expressed in the covenant of the Gospel, were darkly and obscurely offered to the fathers, and were apprehended by their *faith*, in the covenant which God made with them. Yet certainly this covenant, as it is now renewed by the coming of Christ, and by the preaching of the apostles, and evangelists, may justly be called a *New Covenant*, and is truly so called both by the prophets and apostles, for diverse good reasons and considerations.

First, because there is as great difference between this covenant so revealed, and the covenant as it was revealed before Christ's incarnation, as there is between an old dark house built up strong, but yet without any whiting or painting, having very few doors or windows in it, and those either very narrow, or else shut up with boards, or stopped with bricks and mortar, that few can enter in, except such as are already within it; and when they are there they have but small light, and some none at all. There is (I say) as great a difference between the covenant, as it was revealed to the fathers, and the same covenant being now renewed with us, as there is between such as old dark house, and the same house when it is repaired from the very foundation, and is all whited over within and without, all painted and beautified, and trimmed from the roof to the foundation and is made full of fair and wide doors on every side, for all sorts of people to enter into it; and has many large windows made in every room, in which none is stopped up; but all are glazed with pure crystal glass, through which the light of the day, and the bright beams of the sun shine most comfortably. This difference will appear most evidently to us, if we compare the Old and New Testament together, and observe the diversity of revelation.

The covenant which God made with the fathers before Christ, was a sure house built on Christ, and founded on God's eternal truth. It was a safe shelter against all rain and soul weather of affliction, and all storms of temptations, and shrouded the fathers from the scorching heat of an evil conscience, and the fiery flames of hell and the devil's fury. But it had few doors, and those narrow ones, such as few could enter through, in other words, only the natural Israelites, who were all included in it by the promise made to *Abraham*, and those who were circumcised proselytes. The windows of it were few also, and those were the dark promises of Christ, which yielded but little light, shadowed over with types and figures, as with a veil of obscurity. It had no glorious ornaments to allure men a far off; it was not whited, nor painted, nor set forth with variety of pleasant pictures which might delight people. But it rather appeared all bloody with the blood of bulls, goats, rams, and lambs, like a slaughter house, and all black and smoky with the continual offering of burnt offerings and sacrifices, and the smoky fumes of incense. Yes, so many were the ceremonies to be observed, and so heavy and intolerable was the burden of them, that it appeared unto all that passed by, to be rather a shop to work and labor in, a mill to grind in, and an house of correction, then any place of rest, or pleasant and comfortable habitation. But this covenant, as it is now renewed with us under the Gospel, is much altered, and made like an house repaired and renewed throughout from the top to the foundation. The rock of Christ on which it is built, is now set forth in all his glorious colors; all the moss of ceremonies which overgrew and covered him, is taken away; he now shines like ivory, crystal, and adamant, most finely polished. The truth of God in his promises, which is the ground of our faith, is now made manifest and clear by the coming of Christ and by the fulfilling of his word which he spoke from the beginning; and now we dare boldly rely and rest on God's word, in sure hope and confidence that his truth will never fail. The ministerial foundations, in other words, the writings of *Moses* and the prophets, are now by the light of the Gospel changed as it were from rough and unhewn stones, and made like smooth polished marble. The four Gospels are, as it were, four doors made in the four sides of this square house, looking towards the four winds of heaven, ready to receive all men from all the four corners of the earth. The many sermons of Christ and his apostles in the New Testament, are as so many windows, through which as through crystal glass, much heavenly light is conveyed and derived to us, even from heaven, from the throne of God; the sweet promised, and many and diverse gifts of the Spirit, as knowledge, faith, tongues, gifts of healing, prophesying, miracles, and the like, are as pleasant and delightsome pictures and ornaments, able to draw, allure, and delight the hearts of all men. And the many outward blessings of peace and plenty which follow the preaching and profession of the Gospel where it is received, are as it were a glorious painting and whiting, which makes this house glorious a far off, and fills and enflames all that pass by with admiration and love of it. Now there is none so obstinate, nor so strict in speech, but he will grant, that an house so altered and renewed throughout, (as I have before showed) may truly be called, though not another, yet a new house; because it is repaired, renewed, and beautified in all parts, though the foundation and substance of the walls, and the timber are the same. And therefore none can deny that the Covenant of

Grace now under the Gospel, though it is the same in substance and matter with that made to the fathers, and has the same foundation, yet being in this way altered, renewed, and beatified, may justly be called, though not another, yet a *New Covenant* at least, and a *better* covenant.

Secondly, the Covenant of Grace which before God made with *Abraham* and his seed, and which was in force only among the Israelites before the coming of Christ, is now by the preaching of the apostles made with all nations, and all the people of the world are received into it, or at least have it offered to them; and there is free access made to all through the new doors which are now made in every side of the covenant (as is before noted). This is manifest by the very mission of the apostles, and the commission which our Savior Christ gave to them, in these words, "Go teach all nations," (Matt. 28:19).

Now experience teaches us, that when an house is not only repaired, but also enlarged every way, and the foundation of it is stretched out an hundred times more than before, it may truly even in respect of itself be called a new house. And when new inhabitants come to dwell in a house in which they never dwelt before, though the house has been long built, and is old in itself; yet to them it is a new habitation, and men in such cases call their houses new houses. Therefore by the same reason it follows necessarily, that the Covenant of Grace which was made with the fathers, being now by the coming of Christ, the light of the Gospel, and more plentiful gifts of the Spirit, much enlarge, and made capable of all nations, and Christ the foundation of it being stretched out to all the world; it may even in itself be called a new and better covenant. Also in respect of the new people which are received into it, it may be called a New Covenant, though in itself it were in no way altered or enlarged at all.

Thirdly, where the seals of a covenant are made new, and the old are taken away, and where the manner of sealing is altered and quite inverted, there we may call it a New Covenant, though the substance is the same. Experience teaches this; for when a man that has a lease of twenty years in a house, gives it up, and takes another of the same term in more full and plain words, or when on some defect which he finds in his deed of sale, either in the form of conveyance, or in the sealing and the witness, he gives up his former deed, and takes another of the same land sealed with other seals, and testified by other witnesses; this we call a new deed, though the land be the same, and the purchase all one in substance and true meaning. Now it is between the Covenant of Grace now under the Gospel, and the same covenant before the coming of Christ. Though this is the same in substance, and the salvation promised is the same, even that which is only in

Christ. Yet the manner of sealing is much altered and inverted, and the outward seals also. The covenant had before many seals, as circumcision, the Passover, and all the sacrifices, ceremonies, type and figures of the Law. Now it has only two, baptism and the Lord's Supper. The old seals were dark and obscure, and had Christ's image but dimly imprinted into them. The new have a more lively resemblance of Christ. In baptism there is the print of the whole Trinity, *the Father, the Son, and the Holy Ghost.* And the signs in the Lord's Supper are so like unto the body and blood of Christ, that they are called by the same name. Before the Gospel the covenant was first sealed typically by Christ's blood; and at last by the blood itself. Now the covenant is first sealed by the blood of Christ itself, and afterwards, to the end of the world, it is sealed to us by the evident signs and remembrances of Christ's death, given by himself as pledges to us.

The old seals were mutable; the new are unchangeable. The old sealing was much in outward show, and very little inwardly by the Spirit. The new is little in outward show, but more by the inward work of the Spirit. The word of the covenant in now more abundantly written in men's hearts, according to the word of the Lord. This is the New Covenant, "I will put my law in their inward parts, and will write it in their hearts," (Jer. 31:33). Which words are to be understood in this way; not that the fathers had not the word written in their hearts, but that it was not so deeply written, nor in the hearts of so many, as now it is. Wherefore the seals and the manner of sealing being so much renewed, and inverted, we may truly call this a New Covenant. So you see the description of the New Covenant now under the Gospel, and the true reasons why it is called the New Covenant, even when it is compared with the covenant made with the fathers, which was the same in the substance with it.

But if we compare it with the Covenant of Nature, which is the Covenant of Works, and of the Law made with man in the creation; then it must of necessary be called new, because that went before it, and was in the time of man's innocency; this came in after the fall; that promised natural life, this promises spiritual also; that tended to hold up the Old *Adam*, this to build up the new.

So likewise, if this New Covenant of the Gospel is compared with the covenant which God made with Israel in the wilderness, it may truly and must necessarily be called new. For that was a mixed covenant, mixed of the Covenant of Nature and of Grace, and contained in the Law, which is the Covenant of Works; and the faith of the promise which is of the Gospel and of Grace (as has before shown). And therefore in respect of the first part of that covenant which promised life to the doers of the Law, this is truly a New

Covenant, differing in substance from it; and indeed the apostles do call this covenant of the Gospel a New Covenant, especially and chiefly in comparison of these two covenants, even that of pure nature, and that mixed covenant of the Law.

CHAPTER 8: AGREEMENT OF THE COVENANTS

The method and order propounded, which is to be followed in showing how the New and Old Covenants of Grace agree and differ.

Now having largely described the covenant of the Gospel, I proceed, for our better satisfaction, to show more fully, plainly and distinctly, the true agreement and difference which is between the first Covenant of Nature, and the second covenant which is the Covenant of Grace, and between the old and new publishing of the Covenant of Grace.

And first for order's sake I will show how the Covenant of Nature and Grace *agree* and *differ*.

Secondly, because the Covenant of Grace has been solemnly published three diverse ways.

First, more darkly and obscurely to the fathers, from *Adam* until the giving of the Law.

Secondly, after a mixed manner to the Israelites, by the ministry of *Moses*.

Thirdly, now at last most plainly and purely since the coming of Christ in the flesh, by the Gospel preached and published to all nations. I will show how this last publishing of the covenant, which is so glorious, that it is called the New Covenant by a special prerogative, agrees with, and differs from the two former publications made, the one with the fathers, *Adam, Noah, Abraham,* and the rest; the other with the Israelites in the wilderness. The clear knowledge of which things may yield much fruit, profit, and comfort, to the hearts and souls of true Christians.

CHAPTER 9:
A THREE-FOLD AGREEMENT

The three-fold agreement between the Covenant of Nature, which is called the first covenant, and the Covenant of Grace, which is called the second covenant.

First, these two covenants agree between themselves, and that in three respects: *first*, the parties are in substance the same in both covenants. In the first Covenant of Works God was the one party, and *Adam* the other; And in the *second*, the parties are still the same in nature and substance, in other words, God and *Adam*, with all mankind his posterity.

Secondly, they agree in diverse of the promises and conditions. In the first God promised to man life and happiness, Lordship over all the creatures, liberty to use them, and all other blessings which his heart could desire to keep him in that happy estate in which he was created. And man was bound to God to walk in perfect righteousness, to observe and keep God's commandments, and to obey his will in all things which were within the reach of his nature, and so far as was revealed to him. In the second also the promise on God's part is life and happiness, with all blessings to it require

Lordship over the creatures, liberty to use them, and a true right and title to them all, and in *lieu* of these he requires of man perfect righteousness and obedience to his will and law, in every point and title, as our Savior Christ says, (Matt. 5:18).

Thirdly, as the one had seals annexed to it for confirmation, so also has the other. The *seal* of the first covenant was the *Tree of Life*, which if *Adam* had received by taking and eating of it, while he stood in the state of innocency, before his fall, he had certainly been established in that estate for ever; and the covenant being sealed and confirmed between God and him on both parts, he could not have been seduced and supplanted by Satan, as some learned men think, and as God's own words seem to imply, (Gen. 3:22). The seals of the second covenant are the *sacraments*, as circumcision, and such like in the Old Testament, and the sacraments of *baptism*, and the *Lord's Supper* in these days of the Gospel, which whoever has once truly received, and is inwardly circumcised as well as outwardly, and washed with the laver of righteousness, and baptized into Christ, and has true communion with him of his body and blood, that man can never fall, for the seed of God abides in him, (1 John 3:9).

CHAPTER 10:

DIFFERENCES

The difference between the Covenant of Nature and of Grace. The six notable things in which the Covenant of Nature differs from the Covenant of Grace.

But as they agree in these things, so they differ diverse ways. First, though the parties are in substance the same, yet in other respects they differ.

First, in the Covenant of Nature, the parties God and man were friends. God was the Creator, man was his creature made after God's image. God was man's good Lord, and man was God's good servant. God loved man, and man loved God with all his heart; there was not any least occasion of the hatred or enmity between them, but all causes of love. But at making the Covenant of Grace, God and man fell out and became enemies. God was provoked to *just* wrath, and his unchangeable justice required that man should die, and be consumed by the fire of God's just wrath. And man became a rebel, and an enemy, and traitor to God, and had conspired with the devil against his Lord and King. God was to man a consuming fire, and man was as straw and stubble before him, by means of his sinful corruption.

Secondly, in the Covenant of Nature, God revealed himself to man, as one God, Creator and Governor of all things, infinite in power, wisdom, nature, and substance. But in the Covenant of Grace, God revealed himself: *one* infinite God, and *three* persons distinguished, not only a Lord and Creator, but also a merciful Redeemer, not only in unity of essence, but also in *Trinity* of persons.

Thirdly, in the Covenant of Nature God was one party, and man alone was another. But in the Covenant of Grace, God is on *both* sides. God simply consider in his essence, is the party opposite to man. And God the Second Person, having taken on him to be incarnate, and to work man's redemption, was on man's side, and takes part with man, that he may reconcile him to God, by bearing man's sins, and satisfying God's justice for them. Thus they differ in respect of the parties.

Secondly they differ in respect of mediation; for in the Covenant of Nature man needed no mediator to come between God and him; he was pure, upright, and good, created after God's image, the nearer he came to God, the greater was his joy and comfort, God's presence was a delight to him. But in the Covenant of Grace, because man by sin, rebellion, corruption and enmity, was separated and alienated in his mind, nature and disposition from God, therefore man could not come to God to enter into covenant with him, but by a perfect, pure and holy Mediator, infinite in power and favor with God, that he might prevail with him, and pacify his wrath, and yet of man's nature and substance: that in and by the nature which had sinned, satisfaction might be made for sin. Without such a Mediator, there could be no covenant made between God and man. If man, being ever since the fall filthy and corrupt, should in his own person come near to God, who is to him a devouring and consuming fire, be as stubble and straw should presently be consumed, and perish at the presence of God. And therefore in making his covenant, a perfect Mediator is necessarily required, both to come between God and man, and to make perfect satisfaction to God's just Law in the behalf of miserable and sinful men, and to work his reconciliation and atonement.

Thirdly, they exceedingly differ in the promises and conditions. First, the promises of God in the Covenant of Nature, were only *natural* life, and *earthly* happiness, with all blessings necessary to them. But in the Covenant of Grace God promises, over and above natural life and *felicity* on earth, *spiritual* life and *blessings* by the communion of his holy and eternal Spirit; not only the spiritual life of grace in this world, but also of *everlasting glory* in the world to come, in the *presence* of his glorious majesty. Secondly, in the first covenant God did not promise life, but to continue life being before already given. But in the second covenant he promises to raise man from the dust of death and eternal damnation in hell (into which he was fallen head-long by transgression) to the light of life, and the blessedness in heaven, of which his nature was never capable before, no not in the state of innocency. Thirdly, in the first covenant the promised portion and possession, was of the earth and of all visible creatures which were fit to serve for man's use. But in the second covenant God promises heaven, and himself who made the heaven, to be the God, the shield and reward of the faithful, and their portion and inheritance, (Gen. 15:1; Psalm 16:5). Fourthly, in the first covenant God promised and gave to man power over all living creatures, to have them as a lord at his command, and to use them for his delight, and to rule, not to kill and eat them. But in the second covenant God gave them to him for sacrifice, yes and also to serve for his food and nourishment.

The fourth difference arises from the conditions which God requires at the hands of man and on man's behalf, for all these great and wonderful blessings. In the first covenant God required of man perfect righteousness and obedience to his whole Law and will, so far as it was in man's power by nature, and revealed to him, and this he would have man to perform by himself in his own person. But in the second covenant he requires, on man's behalf, a more excellent obedience and righteousness performed to the whole Law more plainly and fully revealed, and greatly enlarged, and that not by man himself or any mere creature, but by the Mediator Jesus Christ, God *and* man in *one* person, who is the end of the law for "righteousness to every one that believeth," (Rom. 10:4).

Now there is wonderful difference between these two. The righteousness required in the first covenant, was only the righteousness of a pure natural man, and able to save him only who performed it; but the righteousness of the second covenant, is the righteousness of a perfect, pure, and holy man filled with the Holy Ghost, which *Adam* did not have in innocency; yes the righteousness of that man, who is one person with God, and so it is the righteousness of God, as the apostle calls it, (2 Cor. 5:21), and is of value to justify not only those who have communion of it, but also a whole world of men besides, if they were made partakers of it. Secondly, the righteousness of the first covenant was only simple actual obedience to the Law, flowing from natural uprightness; but the righteousness of the second, consists of habitual holiness, and of obedience both active and passive to the precepts and penalties, commands and threatenings of the Law; it has in it both the sacrifice of righteousness, and also perfect satisfaction for sin by voluntary submission to sufferings and death.

Thirdly, the righteousness of the first covenant consisted only in obedience to the moral Law. But the righteousness of the second is obedience both to the moral and ceremonial Law. For our Savior Christ was circumcised, presented in the temple, ate the Passover, and observed all the ceremonial ordinances of God, yes and was baptized by *John* (as the Gospel testifies) and that not for himself (for he was free born, without sin, and needed not to offer sacrifice, or to be circumcised or washed) but only to fulfill all righteousness, and to supply the defects of the fathers in their obedience to God's ceremonial ordinances of old, and also our defects in our baptism and other evangelical ordinances: so much he himself testifies (Matt. 3:15; Rom. 15:8).

Fourthly, in the first covenant God did not promise to man a righteousness performed to his hand by a surety and intercessor; but only gave man natural strength and power to perform the righteousness which he require of him; but yet such mutable strength, that the devil by sudden temptation might prevent him before he was confirmed, and so pervert and supplant him. But in the second covenant God gives both the righteousness performed to our hands, and also his Holy Spirit which works in us faith and strength of grace to receive and enjoy it; yes, by dwelling in us as God's immortal seed, unites us to Christ, and bring us to communion of all his benefits, as his sonship, righteousness, satisfaction and the rest, and all this God both promises and gives freely, so that this is *foedus gratiutum*, a most free covenant.

The fifth difference is in the seals; for though in this, both covenants agree, that seals were annexed to them, yet they differ in the seals and manner of sealing, both inward and outward. The seal of the first covenant was the tree of life. But the seals of the second covenant were the Sabbath of the seventh day, sacrifices, circumcision, and the Passover in the old time; and now the sacraments of baptism, and the Lord's Supper. The seal of the first covenant was but a pledge to confirm man in natural life, and in natural belief and assurance. But the seals of the second have the Holy Spirit of God inwardly working with them, and by them.

Lastly, they differ in success, effect, strength, and perpetuity. The first covenant had no good success, it never took effect to save any one of *Adam's* sons; yes it is abolished, only the law and condition of it stands firm in the matter and substance of it (being God's immutable will, and eternal rule of righteousness), in other words, that without perfect obedience to God's revealed will, man shall never come to eternal life, but is under the jaws of death. But the second covenant, being made in such a perfect Mediator, and sealed with the blood of Jesus Christ, God and man, which is of infinite and eternal value, has had good success from the beginning, has taken effect in all ages, and is in force and virtue for ever world without end.

CHAPTER 11:

USE OF THE DOCTRINE

The profitable and holy use which may be made of the doctrine concerning those differences between the Covenant of Nature and the Covenant of Grace.

Now the consideration of these differences serves to show God's infinite mercy and wonderful bounty to miserable man. In that by *Adam's* fall he took occasion to be better to us, and when we were become his enemies, did more exercise and show his goodness, and give greater grace to us. If God had renewed again after man's fall the first covenant of natural life, it had been a great favor. But as if that were but a little in his eyes, he makes a better covenant, even an eternal, and that of better promises, even promises of spiritual life and eternal blessedness in heaven. Also if God and man being by man's fault become utter enemies extremely contrary one to another, God had yielded so far as to accept of a Mediator hired by man to speak for him; surely it had been great mercy and clemency: for we see that earthly kings will admit no intercessors for rebels and traitors, except fear and necessity drive them to it. But God in this point showing mercy beyond all that reason could imagine or expect; when man fled from God, and had no mind, will or inclination to sue for mercy, God sought after him and offered freely to him a Mediator not of the ordinary rank of creatures, but this own Son out of his heart, and that not to speak, plead, or entreat only for man; but also to be incarnate and made man under the law, and subject to the curse of it in man's stead, and by yielding himself voluntarily to a cursed death, to make a full satisfaction for man's sin. O heavens blush, and O earth be astonished at this, to see the Son of God so abased for God's enemies; well might the sun hide his face when this Mediator suffered, as the Gospel testifies, (Matt. 27:45-46). And yet the Lord's bounty does not stay not here; he goes further, and when man neglects and despises his bounty, and neither will nor can desire or seek to be partaker of it, he sends his word to call him, and his Spirit to convert him and change his heart, and not only to make him hunger, and thirst after Christ and his righteousness; but also to unite him to Christ, and to bring him to communion of all his benefits and heavenly treasures. So the more that we have multiplied our rebellion and transgression against God to provoke him to wrath, the more has he magnified his mercy, and enlarged his bounty towards us; and the more that sin has abounded in men, the more has his grace abounded towards them. O let us now at length, when he has done all these things for us, remember ourselves, and turn to him with sorrow and repentance for our sins past, let us labor to redeem the time formerly misspent in vanity, by double thankfulness and obedience; and yet when we have done all we can, let us to his glory profess, that we are unprofitable servants, we have not done half our duty, and if we have any mind to glory and rejoice, let us glory and triumph in the Lord, and give him all laud and praise for ever and ever. We see, then, the manifold wisdom of God *clearly* in his work of salvation through Jesus Christ in covenant theology.

CHAPTER 12:

AGREEMENT IN THE OLD TESTAMENT

The agreement between the Covenant of Grace, as it was revealed to the fathers of the Old Testament; and the same renewed and more fully explained in the Gospel.

After the agreement and difference between the Covenant of Nature and the Covenant of Grace plainly laid open, I proceed to show how the second covenant, in other words, the Covenant of Grace agrees and differs in respect of the diverse publishings and promulgations of in the Old and New Testament. The revelation of it in the Old Testament, I have reduced to two heads: The one is that by which it was revealed to the fathers before the Law, and renewed in diverse ages; as first, to *Adam*, secondly, to *Noah*, thirdly, to *Abraham*, *Isaac*, and *Jacob*; The other is the revealing and renewing of it with Israel in the wilderness, in the giving the law by the ministry of *Moses* after which it continued in one stay until the coming of Christ: With these two my purpose is now to compare the covenant as it is now fully revealed in the Gospel;

And first with the covenant as it was revealed to the fathers before the Law. That Old, and this New agree in diverse ways.

First the parties in general are the same in both covenants. In the covenant with the fathers, the one party was God offended by man's sin, and provoked to wrath and displeasure by his rebellion, and so made a consuming and devouring fire unto him. And the other party was man by means of his fall and corruption now made a rebel and enemy unto God, and as stubble and dross before his presence. And in the covenant, as it is revealed in the Gospel, the parties are still the same, even God offended, and man the sinner and offender.

Secondly, they agree in this, that a Mediator is required in both between the parties God and man so far separated, and standing at so great a distance, for to make up the breach and the league between them, being at so great odds. And both have one Mediator, Jesus Christ the promised seed, who alone in heaven and earth is able to stand before the devouring fire, and to make atonement between God and man. For that seed of the woman which in the first making of the covenant was promised to *Adam* to break the serpent's head, (Gen. 3:15) that seed which was promised to *Abraham* and *Isaac*, in whom all the nations of the earth should be blessed,

(Gen. 12 and 22) that Shiloh which *Jacob* spake of in his blessing of *Judah*, (Gen. 49). He was the Mediator in the covenant between God and the fathers before the Law; and he is no other but *Jesus Christ*, who came in the fullness of time; who by having his heel bruised in this sufferings, has broken the serpent's head, that is destroyed the works of the devil, who by his apostles, (Gal. 3:9) has called all nations to the participation of *Abraham's* blessing, and to justification by faith in him. He was made and born of a woman a pure virgin by the power of the Holy Spirit, (Luke 1:35) and "is now and ever hath been, yesterday and today and the same for ever, a perfect redeemer and eternal Mediator of the covenant now under the Gospel," (John 8:56, 24:6; Eph. 4:16; Heb. 13:8).

Thirdly, in both these covenants the substance of the promises is one and the same. As we have the promise of spiritual life by the communion of the Holy Spirit, both of the life of grace in this world, and of the eternal life of glory in the world to come; so all the fathers had this from the beginning. As we have the promise of a true right and title to all earthly blessings also in Christ; so they had this also. As God is given to us in Christ to be our portion, so he by *covenant* gave himself to them to be their God. As we have Christ God and man give to us to be our Savior, and his righteousness and obedience, with all the merits of his death, to be apprehended by faith for our justification, so had they from the first time of the promise. All this the apostle shows most plainly, (Heb. 11) where he shows that the forefathers did by faith not only receive earthly blessings, as the land of Canaan, deliverance from enemies and oppressors, safety from the flood; but also they embraced the promises of a better life, and of a better country, even an heavenly, "and God is not ashamed to be called their God, for he hath prepared for them a city," (Heb. 11:16). "They received Jesus Christ by faith, and did so firmly believe in him, that they esteemed reproach for his sake greater riches then all earthly treasures," (Heb. 11:26); "They by faith became heirs of his righteousness," (Heb. 11:7); "We (the apostle says) believe to be saved by the grace of our Lord Jesus Christ , even as they," (Acts 15:11).

Fourthly, the covenant made with the fathers *agrees* with the covenant now under the Gospel, in one and the same condition of man's behalf, in other words, the perfect righteousness of the Law, and perfect obedience to the whole revealed will of God, performed not by every believer himself, but by his Mediator Jesus Christ, God and man, in man's nature. This righteousness as made theirs, and is made ours by one and the same means, even by communion of the Spirit, and by true faith laying hold upon it, applying it, and offering it up to God. Both the righteousness and the means by which it is made ours, are free gifts and graces of God both to the fathers and us. Neither they were, nor we are sufficient of ourselves, or fit to perform any thing for salvation, or to receive salvation when it is offered freely; all our will, all our sufficiency, and all our fitness is of God, and ever has been. And therefore howsoever Christ his righteousness and satisfaction made to God in the nature of man, may in respect of Christ our head be called a condition of salvation which God required on man's behalf: yet in respect of us and the fathers also, it is rather a part of the blessing, and one of the free promises in the covenant, and at our hands God requires no condition at all, but such as he himself freely of his grace performs and works in us and for us. And therefore as the covenant which God has now made with us, so also that covenant with the fathers before the Law was *fadus gratuitum*, a free Covenant of Grace.

Fifthly, the covenants both Old and New agree in the seals diverse ways.

First, as in the Old, so in this New, outward seals and signs are required for to seal and confirm them.

Secondly, as their seals signified the shedding of Christ's blood, and his cursed death for man's sin, also mortification and sanctification; so do the seals of baptism and the Lord's Supper, which are annexed to our covenant. As their seals both taught the manner of man's redemption, and also served to confirm their faith in it, so do ours both set before us Christ's death and obedience, and our communion with him and also *confirm* our faith and confidence in him. As their sacraments were parts of their profession, and were testimonies of their love to God, and were accounted God's worship, so are ours. As their sacraments distinguished them from pagans, infidels, and all strange sects, so do ours. As their sacraments had God as their author, so ours. Ours and theirs are *both* seals of the righteousness of faith, *both* are effectual to believers only, *both* have the same effects, increase of faith, hope, confidence, love, charity among men, and the like. So far these two covenants agree in their seals.

Lastly, they agree in the general success, effect, and sufficiency; for both of them have had good success, and taken effect, and been sufficient to give birth to grace in the elect, and to bring all true believers to eternal salvation and blessedness. The covenant plainly revealed in the Gospel, brings all *true* Christians to believer in Christ, and to find comfort and salvation in his mediation, intercession, righteousness, resurrection, and victory over death. So by the covenant made of the Old with the fathers, *Adam, Abel, Enoch,* and *Noah,* were brought to believe in Christ, and were saved. *Enoch* by faith in Christ was translated; *Noah* by faith made the ark to the saving of himself and his household; *Abraham* saw by faith the day of Christ, and by believing in him was justified; *Job* rejoiced that Christ God would plead for man with God, and the Son of man for his friend and neighbor, (Job 16:21), and professed his faith and confidence in the resurrection of Christ *his* Redeemer, (Job 19:25).

CHAPTER 13:
SEVEN DIFFERENCES

The seven-fold differences between the Covenant of Grace, as it was made with the fathers, and the covenant as it was made in the Gospel.

They differ in diverse ways. The first, which is indeed the greatest difference of all, is the respect of the darkness and obscurity of the one, and the plainness and perspicuity of the other. The covenant with the fathers was every way, and in every point more dark and obscure, involved in types and shadows of Christ. The covenant in the Gospel is plain and perspicuous, it removes the veil, and shows Christ's substance with an open face. In the Old Covenant the severity of God's justice, and his just wrath and enmity against sin did not so plainly appear, because the effect of them was not made manifest on his own dear Son our Mediator, until he came to suffer actually such ignominy, reproach, agonies, and a most ignominious and cursed death for our sins which he took upon him to bear, and which were imputed to him, and punished in him our surety. God's not sparing him, but afflicting him with all his storm, and delivering him up to hellish pains and agonies, and to a cursed death, do wonderfully show his infinite wrath against sin, which was darkly revealed to the fathers in types and figures in the slaughter of beasts, and burning of sin offerings. So likewise, though in the Old Testament we read of God, and some mention of his Son, (Psalm 2:12; Prov. 30:4), and of the Spirit of God, and find many phrases which signify *more* persons than one or two in one *Jehovah,* yet the mystery of the Trinity was not so fully revealed, as now it is in the Gospel, in which we have plain affirmation of *three distinct persons*, the Father, the Son, and the Holy Spirit, in the unity of God's essence, and all the three are said to be one, though by distinct properties and diverse works they are described to us severally, and distinguished one from another. And by this we see that the New Covenant of the Gospel is more plain, and the Old more dark, in respect of the parties God and man between whom the covenants are made.

Secondly, in the Old, Christ the Mediator was darkly shadowed out to the fathers; they had only this knowledge of Christ, that they should be saved by a Mediator, that this Mediator should be the seed of the woman, that he should be the Archangel or Prince of angels, and Emmanuel, God with us, (Isa. 7 and 9), yes, and should be called the mighty God, and should make atonement for sin, and bring in eternal righteousness, (Dan. 9). But how God and man should in him become one person, how God in him should be incarnate and humbled, and stand in our place, and bear our sins, how he should fulfill the law in every particular point, how he should satisfy justice, and suffer the wrath of God; these things were not distinctly, nor fully revealed to them, only the extraordinary prophets had some foresight of them, and did more plainly at sometimes describe some of them. But now in the Gospel we see the person of our Savior, and his two natures most plainly set forth before us, the manner of his obedience, death, and satisfaction, and the particular uses of them, as also the virtue of his resurrection and ascension. And therefore the New Covenant is more plain in respect of the Mediator. Thirdly, all the promises of eternal life and salvation, and the condition on man's behalf, how and after what manner it should be performed; also the things signified and confirmed by the seals, were far more dark and obscure in the Old Covenant. But in the New Covenant of the Gospel, all these things are so plain, that even children may learn and understand them. And thus in all respects, and in all parts the Old was more obscure, and the New is more plain. And this is the first, and the main difference. Out of this there arise two others, even a second and third difference between these covenants.

The one which is the second in order, is a difference in the parties received into the covenants. The Old Covenant, because of dimness and obscurity, did shine forth but a little, and gave light only to them who were near at hand; and on this it came to pass that it reached to a very few; sometimes but to one or two families, and when it was in greatest force, but to on nation and people of the world. But the New Covenant in brightness of knowledge, and plainness of revelation shines like the sun, and gives light far and near to all nations, even to them that sat in darkness, and in the shadow of death. And on this it comes to pass, that people of all nations are received into this covenant, and the parties which now enter league with God, are not some few men, or one nation, but all nations and people of the world, God is one party, and all nations of the earth are the other party.

A third difference consists in the power, efficacy, success, and effect which is diverse in these two covenants; for however they agree in these generally, because both of them have had success, taken effect, and been of power to bring many to salvation (as it before noted); yet by reason of the obscurity of the Old, it has taken less effect, and been of less power. And the New by means of plainness and light, has brought with it more excellent gifts, and more abundance of grace to many, and has been of greater force, power, and efficacy, and the Spirit has wrought more powerfully by it. For faith (as the apostle says), which is, as it were, the root of other graces, "cometh by hearing, and hearing by the word,"

(Rom. 10:17), where the word is more plainly preached and heard with understanding, there must necessarily be greater knowledge and faith, and there these the Spirit must necessarily work more powerfully and effectually, and show all graces more abundantly in the hearers. On this it comes to pass, that the Old Covenant worked weakly in all, except those that were extraordinarily called and enlightened, because of its obscurity, and unfitness to give birth to knowledge and faith. But by virtue of the *New* the Lord writes his Law in our hearts, and makes us all know him more fully, as he did with Abraham (Jer. 31:33), and pours out his Spirit with *abundance* of grace on all flesh, (Joel 2:28).

A fourth difference is in the circumstance of the promises and gifts, the Old Covenant promised life and salvation in Christ, who then was *to come.* And Christ who is the foundation of all the promises, though he had then taken on him to work man's redemption, and his future death and obedience were actually in force from the beginning, able to save all believers; yet he was not actually come in the flesh, neither had *actually* performed these things for man. But the New Covenant promises salvation and all blessings in Christ being already come in the flesh. And Christ has actually performed all things which were needful for our redemption, and we are by the New Covenant made partakers of his sacrifice already offered, and his righteousness already performed for us.

A fifth difference arises from the order and mixture of the promises. The Old Covenant first and chiefly promised earthly and temporal blessings, as deliverance from bodily enemies and dangers, and plenty of worldly good, as houses, lands, wealth, riches, increase of children, length of days and such like, and in and under these it signified and promised all spiritual blessings, and salvation. But the New Covenant promises *Christ* and his *spiritual* blessings in the first place, and after them earthly blessings. First it brings us to the kingdom of God, and the righteousness of it, and then it ministers other things to us. Again the Old Covenant abounded in earthly promises of worldly blessings, but had few promises of spiritual and heavenly blessedness intermingled; but the new insists almost altogether on heavenly rewards, and promises of spiritual blessings, and has but few promises of temporal and worldly good things. And so both the order of the promises, and the unequal mixture of earthly and heavenly blessings, make another difference between the Old and New Covenant.

Sixthly, they differ in the outward matter of the seals, the outward rites, and in the order of sealing. The seals of the Old Covenant were many, and those laborious, costly, heavy, and burdensome; circumcision was painful, sacrifices were costly, and the many oblations, offerings, and purifications, were a burden too heavy for the fathers to bear. But the seals of the New are few, and but two, the least number that can be, and those very easy without toil or cost, or pain of body or mind. The matter of the old seals were oxen, sheep, goats, birds, incense, odors, calves, lambs, cutting of the flesh, shedding of the blood, burning, and killing of diverse creatures. The matter of the new seals is only water sprinkled, and bread and wine broken, poured out, distributed, eaten, and drunken, and this is all that the seals differ much in outward matter; also in the order of sealing. The Old was first typically sealed with shadows, and after with the substance, Christ's body and blood. The New was sealed first with Christ's blood and death, and is now sealed by the outward signs daily in the sacrament.

Lastly, they differ in perpetuity. For though the substance of both is one and the same, eternal and unchangeable; yet the form and manner of making and sealing is changeable in the Old, but is the New perpetual. The Old Covenant has new words added to it, even the New Testament; and the outward seals are abolished, and new put in their place. But to the words of the New Covenant no more plain words shall be added, neither shall the outward seals of it be altered, but shall remain until the coming of the Lord. And therefore the Old is but in *substance* only; but the New is in *all respects* perpetual and unchangeable. So much both of the agreement and the difference between the Old and New Covenant of Grace.

CHAPTER 14:
TWO-FOLD USE

A two-fold use is made of the doctrine in the two former chapters.

First, the agreement which is between two covenants of Grace, serves to assure us, that all the faithful forefathers, from the beginning, did partake of the same graces with us, and had fellowship and communion of the same spirit, with one and the same Jesus Christ, and were justified by his righteousness, and saved eternally by faith in him, even as we are at this day. If sin in them could have hindered the work of God's grace, so it might do in us, for we are sinners as well as they, and God has a just quarrel against us. If our Mediator is of power to save eternally, then must they also necessarily be saved as well as we; for they had the *same* Christ. He was yesterday, is today, and shall be the same *forever*. If God's promise is true, and if they cannot fail, surely they had the same in substance which we have. If salvation rests on the condition of righteousness, they had the same which we have, even the righteousness of God in Christ, and by the same faith they partook of it. If seals can help anything at all, they had them also as well as we. And if we may judge of the power of the covenant, by the success and effect in some persons, we shall find that *Enoch* and *Elijah* were by the grace of the Old Covenant saved even from bodily death, and taken up into heaven and happiness. And therefore let this consideration of the unity and agreement which is between the New and Old Covenant of Grace, admonish us not to be puffed up with pride, and a false concept; as if we only under the Gospel were respected of God, and saved by faith in Jesus Christ. Let this teach us to think reverently of the fathers in the old time, and love and reverence the name and remembrance of them as saints glorified in heaven, spiritual members of the same Christ, and partakers of the same grace with us. But above all let this enflame our hearts with a deadly hatred and detestation of all those heretics, and their doctrine, as the Manicheans, Anabaptists, antinomians, blasphemous Servetus, and the rest who have not been ashamed to teach boldly that the fathers never partook of saving grace in Christ, neither were under the same covenant of Life with us; but only were fed with temporal promises, and earthly blessings, as hogs and calves for slaughter. And let us count the popish fiction of *limbus partum*[2] a doting dream, justly to be abhorred of all true Christians as a *loathsome abomination.*

---

[2] In Roman Catholicism this refers to a "region" between heaven and hell, the dwelling place of souls not condemned to punishment but deprived of the joy of existence with God in heaven. Walker here refers to *limbus patrum*

Secondly, the differences noted between the Old, and New Covenant of Grace, serve to magnify in our eyes God's extraordinary love and bounty towards us who now live in the light of the Gospel. Though the fathers were fed with the true bread of life, yet in a small measure, and more coarse manner prepared; and though the light of life shined to them, yet it was dimly through clouds and mists. The taste and sight which they had of Christ in this life increased their hunger more, then satisfy their appetite, and increased more their thirst after him. They had few examples, and present patterns of holy men to follow; the number of believers was small, and so there were but few helps and encouragements in true religion. The gifts of the Spirit were rare, scarce to be found in two or three among a great multitude; and those gifts of knowledge, faith, and heavenly wisdom, which those few had, were small, and not so eminent. But the Lord has opened to us the windows and floodgates of heaven, and rained down more abundantly all blessings on our heads; he has made the river of life, which makes glad the city of God (Psalm 46:4), and makes flow among us such things in full streams; he has fed us to the full with the bread of life, so that hypocrites begin like Israel to loath his heavenly manna. We live in the glorious

---

("fathers' limbo"), where Old Testament saints were confined until liberated by Jesus in his "descent into hell." This is complete heresy and blasphemy against the covenant of God and work of Jesus Christ.

light, and see Christ clearly. We have many examples of godly men on every side round about us to provoke us, many patterns to work by; much encouragement, plenty of all gifts of learning, knowledge, wisdom, faith, love, and the like. Now how comes this to pass? Is it because we are better than our forefathers, or because we have better deserved? Surely in no case; for they were by many degrees more excellent in natural gifts then we, less rebellious, and more ready to make good use of small means, then we are of greatest. Which of us dares compare with *Enoch, Noah, Abraham,* or *David?* As the world grows old, and we grow weak in bodily strength, and low in stature; so we still grow more and more strong in corruption and in forwardness of heart; And the Lord's mercy and bounty is so much grater to us then to them, because we are further from deserving any mercy then they were, and do deserve more misery. The only thing in which we are better than they, is this; that the Lord has *shown* more goodness to us than them. Therefore, let us all confess and say to the glory of God, that it is his mercy not our merit, to him belongs all the praise. "It is not of him that willeth, nor in him that runneth, but in God that showeth mercy," (Rom. 9:16). To him be glory and honor for ever world without end.

CHAPTER 15:

THE COVENANT WITH MOSES

The agreement between the pure and plain Covenant of Grace in the Gospel, and the mixed covenant which God made with Israel on Mount Horeb, by the ministry of Moses, which consisted partly of the Covenant of Works, and partly the Covenant of Grace.

Now having laid down the agreement, and difference between the New and Old Covenant of Grace, that is, the covenant as it was made with the fathers before the Law, and the covenant as it is now plainly published in the Gospel, it follows now that I should show the agreement and difference between the same pure and plain Covenant of Grace in the Gospel, and the mixed covenant which God made with Israel on Mount Horeb by the ministry of *Moses* which consisted partly of the Covenant of Works, and partly of the Covenant of Grace (as is before noted). If I should insist on all the differences and agreements which are between these two covenants, I should repeat all the agreements and differences which I have before declared to be between the Covenant of Nature and of Grace, and also between the Old Covenant of Grace and the New. For the first part of the covenant which

God made with Israel at Horeb, was nothing else but a *renewing* of the Old Covenant of Works which God made with *Adam* in paradise. And the second part which God made with them, first obscurely when he gave them by *Moses* the Levitical Laws, and ordained the tabernacle, the ark, and the mercy seat, which were *types* of Christ; and secondly more plainly in the plains of *Moab* which is far down in the book of Deuteronomy; this was nothing else but a renewing of the Covenant of Grace which he had before made with their fathers, *Adam, Abraham, Isaac,* and *Jacob.* And therefore the same agreements which I have before showed to be between the Covenant of Nature and of Grace, the same are between the first part of the covenant which God made at Mount Sinai, and the covenant under which we now live in the Gospel. Likewise there are the same differences, only one excepted; for where in the first Covenant of Nature God and man were friends, both just and righteous, both lovers, and neither of them offended; now in renewing the same covenant with Israel, the parties were in variance, for God was provoked to wrath, and man by sin was become an enemy, even as they were at the making of the Covenant of Grace.

In like manner, if we consider the second party of the covenant made with Israel, it being the same with the Old Covenant of Grace, we shall find between it and the New

Covenant of the Gospel, the same agreements and differences which I have last before showed to be between the Old and New Covenant of Grace. Wherefore I will now take the whole covenant which God made with all Israel by the ministry of *Moses*, as it consists of both these parts jointly together, and so I will compare it with the covenant of the Gospel, and show the agreement and difference between them.

And first for the things in which they agree, besides those before named, in which the parts of the covenant made with Israel, do agree with the covenant of the Gospel, I find but two only. First, they agree in the main and principal end, namely the revelation of the glory of the goodness, justice, and mercy of God in man's salvation; at this they both aim, and in this they both agree. Secondly, they both agree in this, that both of them do promise to us justification and salvation in Christ, and both require in us a continual endeavor to fulfill the whole Law, as near as we can every man in his own person. For although Christ is the end and fulfilling of the Law for righteousness to all true believers; yet after that we are justified by his righteousness, it is required in every one of us, that we should labor to avoid every sin against the Law, and do all holy duties which the Law requires, so far as we are able. This we promise in baptism; and whosoever willfully lives, and continues in any sin, and purposely abstains from good when occasion is offered, and omits holy duties which the law requires, as observing of the Sabbath, hearing of the word, and such like, we count him a carnal man, and he has no part as yet in the Covenant of Grace. For he that is justified, is also mortified, and sanctified, and cannot purposely continue in any sin of omission or commission.

CHAPTER 16:
A PURE AND MIXED COVENANT

The several differences between the pure and mixed covenant.

But the differences between them are many and great. First, they differ in the manner of requiring obedience to the Law, and exacting good works. The covenant of *Moses* requires, that a man should first endeavor to fulfill the whole law, that by this he may be justified, and live; and if he cannot do so, that then he should fly to sacrifices for sin, and free-will offerings, and in them, as in types, to Christ and his righteousness and obedience, that there he may find that which by the Law he cannot obtain. But the covenant of the Gospel requires that a man should first renounce himself, and all his own righteousness, and seek salvation and righteousness in Christ by faith, and that being justified by grace in Christ, he should by way of thankfulness labor to the utmost, to bring forth all fruits of holiness, righteousness, and obedience to all God's commandments, and that for this end, that he may glorify God, adorn his profession, and be more and more assured of his communion with Christ, and sincere love to God.

Secondly, these covenants differ in matter and substance. The matter and substance of the covenant made by the ministry of *Moses*, it was mixed, it was partly conditional, and partly absolute; partly *legal*, and partly *evangelical*; it required to justification both works and faith, but after a diverse manner, and it was a mixed covenant of two diverse covenants, both the Covenant of Works, and the Covenant of Grace.

First, it required works, that men should do the works of the Law and live and this it did by way of the first covenant. For the *Moral Law* written in two tables of stone, and consisting of the Ten Commandments which God spoke from Mount Sinai, is called by the name of a covenant, "He declared to you (*Moses* says there) his covenant which he commanded you to perform, even Ten Commandments, and he wrote them upon two tables of Stone," (Deut. 4:13), and "These two table are called the tables of the covenant," (Deut. 9:9); by these testimonies it is plain that the law was given to Israel as a covenant which required obedience for justification and life.

Secondly, this covenant given by *Moses*, promised Christ, and required that whoever they failed in their obedience to the Law, they should flee to sacrifices and sin offerings, which were types of Christ, and did prefigure, signify and seal his satisfaction and atonement for sin, and that by faith they should seek righteousness and satisfaction in him, and should rest on those promises which God made with their fathers, that in Christ the blessed seed all nations of the earth should be blessed. And this is the second, even the evangelical part of the covenant, and is called by the name of another covenant, (Deut. 29:2). For indeed this is the Covenant of Grace, as the other part is the Covenant of Works. This God propounds absolutely, the other is conditional, that a man shall do it if he can, and if he can do it shall live; if he cannot, that he should flee by faith to Christ, foreshadowed in types, and promised to the fathers. So the covenant which God made with Israel, was not a simple, but a mixed covenant, and the matter of it was mixed. But the Covenant of Grace in the Gospel is simple without mixture, and propounds no other way to salvation, but only in and through Jesus Christ; no justification but that which is by faith in Christ's obedience, without our own works. This is a second difference.

The rest of the main differences are plainly laid down by the Apostle *Paul*, (2 Cor. 3). One is, that the covenant which God made with Israel, was an Old Covenant. For it is called by the apostle διαθήκη (*diatheke*), (2 Cor. 3:14). But the covenant made with all nations by the Gospel, is called καινῆς διαθήκης, the *New Covenant*, (2 Cor. 3:6). Now the covenant with Israel may truly be called Old, and is so indeed in respect of the covenant under the Gospel, for two reasons.

First, because the legal part of it, which was the *Covenant of Works* laid down in the Ten Commandments of the Law written in tables of stone, is in substance all one with the first covenant which God made with man in the state of innocency; the sum of both is that one thing, "Do this and live."

Secondly, because the evangelical part of it, which promised life and righteousness in Christ the promised seed, was given after the old manner, as it was to the fathers before the Law, that is, in general, dark and obscure promises, and showed Christ only afar off, to come in the later ages of the world. But the covenant of the Gospel is every way *new*. It is made with us after a *new* manner; it shows Christ *already* come, and that most plainly, and it has *no relics of the Old Covenant of Works* in it, but teaches justification by faith *without works*, even by communion of Christ and of his righteousness alone, *without any concurrence of our own righteousness and works of the Law concurring for justification.*

Another difference which the apostle makes between these covenants, is, that the one is the letter, the other the

Spirit; for so he affirms (2 Cor. 3:6). Now the reasons of this are two especially: The first reason why the covenant with Israel is called the letter and the covenant of the Gospel the Spirit, is because *Moses* who was the mediator of the covenant with Israel, gave only the letter of the covenant, that is, that Law and the covenant written in tables and in letters, but he could not give the Spirit to make them understand the covenant, nor any inward grace and ability to make them keep it. But Christ the Mediator, by whose ministry the covenant of the Gospel is given, has also the Holy Spirit in himself without measure, which Spirit be by his word, and together with the word of the covenant, sends into our hearts, and enables us to believe and to keep the covenant. And as *John* the Baptist, comparing himself and his ministry with the ministry of Christ, saith, "I baptize you with water, but he shall baptize you with the Holy Ghost and with fire," (Matt. 3:11); that is, "I give only the *outward* sign, but he gives the *inward* grace." So it may be said of *Moses* and *Christ*, that *Moses* gave only the letter or writing of the covenant; but Christ gives the word, and with the Spirit of grace also, which makes it *effectual* to salvation. And therefore the covenant, as it proceeds from *Moses*, and comes by his *ministry*, is but a *letter*; but that which Christ gave as Mediator, is the *Spirit*.

Another reason may be drawn from the manner of giving. *Moses* gave the covenant written in letters which many could see, but could not read; and many could read, and could not understand; and many could understand literally, after a natural and carnal manner according to the proper literal sense, but they could not understand the words *spiritually* according to the *spiritual sense*, they could not see nor discern the true *scope, end,* and *use* of the words. But Christ preached the covenant of the Gospel, by a lively voice, in words easy to be understood, which did not only sound in the ears, but also pierce into the hearts and spirits of the hearers, and not only showed the matter, but also the manner, end, and use of everything, and how the Law and Commandments do not only bind the outward man, and require the outward act, but also do bind the inward man, even the soul and spirit, and do require all holy thoughts, motions, and dispositions of the heart and soul. And so the words of the New Covenant are fit instruments of the Spirit, and the Spirit works powerfully by them.

Another difference laid down by the apostle, (2 Cor. 3:13, 14, 18), is, that there was a veil before the covenant with Israel, which hindered their sight, so that the people could not look into the end, nor see the right use of the Law and the ceremonies of it. But the covenant of the Gospel is given with much evidence of speech, and in this we all with open face behold, as in a glass, the glory of the Lord. Now this veil consisted of two parts: The first was the darkness and blindness of their hearts, and the weakness of their sight. The second was the obscurity and darkness of the covenant itself, which both in respect of the words, and also of the seals, the types and figures, was very dark, and hard to be understood. First, the people themselves were naturally by reason of original corruption blind and ignorant, and not able to see the right end and use of the Law and covenant; yes, their fight was so weak, that they could no more look on God's glory, then the weak eye of a man can look on the bright sun when it shines in full strength; and therefore being not able to look on the glory of God shining in the covenant, they could in no case see into the end and use of it. So their own weakness and blindness was a veil to them, and is this day to all the Jews, until their hearts are converted to the Lord, (2 Cor. 3:16), and until he pours out his Spirit on them. Secondly, the words of the covenant were spoken, and the seals and ceremonies ordained after such an obscure manner, that a veil of darkness hung over them, until Christ by his actual fulfilling of the Law, and by the words of the New Covenant in the Gospel, made all *plain*, and pulled away the veil of darkness. This obscurity of the covenant proceeded from three special causes; the first was God's hiding and concealing of his purpose in the giving of the Law. For his purpose in giving the moral Law, was not that Israel should do it and be justified by it, which after man's fall and corruption is *impossible*; but only to teach them and us what is true and perfect righteousness which leads to life, and to make all men examine themselves by it as by a rule; that by it finding themselves destitute of righteousness, and utterly unable to perform righteousness, they might be driven out of themselves, and so prepared to receive Christ, and embrace his righteousness. Also God's purpose and counsel in giving the ceremonial law, was not that men should perform them as any part of righteousness to justification; neither did he ordain them to be of themselves purgations from sin, and expiations of iniquity, but only to be types foreshadowing Christ, and his all-sufficient sacrifice, and seals of the covenant which sealed it, not by any virtue in them, but by virtue of *Christ's blood* which they signified. Now though this was God's counsel and purpose in giving the Law moral and ceremonial, yet he did conceal, and not in plain words express it; he did not tell them that he meant by putting them on the performances of the Law, to make them find out their own weakness and insufficiency, and on this flee to Christ, the end of the Law, and the substance of the ceremonies and sacrifices.

But contrarily he required their *performance* of the Law for the obtaining of life, and so spoke as though it had been possible for them to fulfill it, and to be justified by it; and so they commonly understood his words, erroneously, even as the papists do at this day, thinking that God would never have commanded them to do the Law, if he had not known that it was in their power to do it, as he commanded; and this was the first cause of the obscurity of that covenant.

The second cause, was the mixture of the legal part of the covenant with the evangelical, and the joining of them both as it were in one continued speech. For first God required by the moral law, that they should do it for the obtaining of life; then immediately he adds to it the ceremonial law, and ordained sacrifices for sin (which did declare them to be sinners, and so destitute of righteousness) and gave them diverse types and shadows of Christ, and by that Law he required obedience and doing, on pains of death and cutting off, so that the people of Israel did still imagine themselves to be in the Covenant of Works; and from that manner of speech used by God, and from the title of laws and statutes which God gave to the ceremonies, and from the words before going, they gathered that the sacrifices, oblations, and other rites were rather laws to be observed for righteousness, then seals of the Covenant of Grace, and signs of Christ and his righteousness; they thought the use of them to consist in doing, not in signifying, and stirring up of faith to lay hold on Christ: and this was a second cause of the darkness of the covenant.

The third cause was the great penury, and scarcity of evangelical promises in that covenant, and the great inequality and disproportion which was between them and the legal commandments of works. For in that covenant we find few promises of life and salvation, but only on condition of works. Christ is very seldom pointed at in plain words. The evangelical promises as they are rare and very few in all the books of the Law which God gave them by *Moses*; so they are either very general, or else very obscure, more then those which were given to the fathers long before: But the legal commandments and promises are many, and those very plain in every place.

And this was a special cause which made the people of Israel to misconstrue the meaning of that covenant, and to think that all salvation was to be obtained by works; and so the covenant was obscure, and the end of it was hid from their sight, they could not understand the true use of the types and ceremonies. But the covenant of the Gospel is made in such plain words, and after such a lively manner sets forth Christ and his perfect ransom, satisfaction, and righteousness to us, and the true way to justification and salvation by faith in him, that the most simple may understand it; and with the plain doctrine and multitude of promises the Spirit of God works powerfully, and is given by Christ in such measure to all sorts of people, that the darkness of their hearts is abolished also, and so there is no veil, neither over their hearts, nor over the covenant itself; but as Christ is plainly offered in the Word, so their hearts are enlightened and enable to look on his glory, and they are transformed into the same image; and on this there comes to be great difference in this respect between the covenant of the Law which God gave by *Moses*.

From these two last differences, there arise others which are there laid down by the apostle also; in other words, that the Old Covenant of the Law is the *ministry of death*, but the covenant of the Gospel is the *ministry of the Spirit and of life*, (2 Cor. 3:7). The Old is the occasion of *sin*, and so the ministry of *condemnation*; the New, of *righteousness* to *justification*. The Old brings *bondage*, the New *liberty*. The Old is *less glorious*, and yet *dazzled* the eyes of the Israelites, that they could not look on it steadfastly; The New is *full of glory*, and yet we can behold in it with *open face* the glory of God, (2 Cor. 3:18). These particular differences are all named and noted by the apostle, and they arise from the two last going before. For reason tells us, that because the Old Covenant was given by the ministry of *Moses* a frail man, and was dark and obscure, subject to be misconstrued, and was not plainly preached by lively voice, but only written in dead letters in the tables of stone; therefore it was no fit instrument for the Spirit to work by; the Spirit did not work by it such plenty of knowledge, faith, and other graces. It only showed them what they should do, but enabled them not to do anything, rather made them more sinful, in provoking their corrupt nature which more lusts after evils forbidden; and it made their sins more willful, which before were done in ignorance; and so it became the ministry of sin, death, and condemnation to them. It also brought them into bondage, by showing them their slavish condition, and giving them no grace to flee from that miserable estate. It dazzled their eyes, because it showed them the glorious majesty and justice of God; but did not give them the grace of the Spirit, to strengthen their sight, to look with boldness and comfort on God's majestical justice. But because the covenant of the Gospel is made in plain words, and given by a Mediator who has also the disposing of the Spirit, and dispensing of spiritual grace; therefore it is a fit instrument for the Spirit to work by, and the Spirit goes forth in great power, by, and with the publication of it, which regenerates men, and renews their hearts, knits them into one body with Christ, gives them the communion of all his righteousness and obedience to justification of life, free them from all fear and bondage, makes them run freely and willingly in the way to life, and in the paths of God's commandments;

enables them to stand boldly before the glorious tribunal of God's justice, and gives them an heavenly eye-salve to their sight, that they may steadfastly behold God's glory in the face of Jesus Christ. And so in those respects those two covenants do differ much between themselves.

The last difference is named by the apostle in 2 Cor. 3:11, and it is this, that the covenant of the Law given by *Moses*, and the glory of it vanishes, and is done away. But the covenant of the Gospel, and the glory of it abides forever. This difference is to be understood, not that the substance of the Law, or the righteousness of it ceases at any time, neither that the evangelical promises which were intermingled in that covenant, are abolished together with the types and ceremonies. These things are in no case to be granted. For the Law of God is an eternal rule of truth and justice, and by the righteousness, obedience, and fulfilling of it all the elect shall be justified, and saved for ever. This our Savior testifies, saying, "Think not that I am come to destroy the Law but to fulfill it; for verily, until heaven and earth pass, not one jot or tittle of the Law shall pass," (Matt. 5:17). Also his blessed apostle, "Do we then make void the Law through faith? God forbid; yea, we establish the Law," (Rom. 3:31), and "Christ is the end or fulfilling of the Law for righteousness to every believer," (Rom. 10:4). And if we rightly consider the ceremonies and the promises given to Israel, we shall perceive that Christ was the body and substance of them all; and therefore so long as he abides, the substance of them abides firm and sure, and does not vanish. Wherefore the Law and covenant which God gave by *Moses* vanishes and is abolished only in three respects.

First, in respect of the extreme *rigor* of it; for as it was given to Israel it required obedience of every man in his own person to justification and life; but now it only requires that a man have that righteousness which is a perfect conformity to it, though performed by his surety and mediator, and that shall sufficiently save him. Before it required *perfect* righteousness, on pain of *damnation, performed by every man himself*, and threatened a curse to *every* breach of it. Now it binds a man himself to perform no more than he is able; if he does his best, and brings a willing mind, God accepts the will for the deed; because now we are *not* to obey the Law for justification; *Christ has done that for us.* Now we are to obey it in *thankfulness* and in *imitation* of Christ, that we may be conformable to his *image*, and by holiness made fit to see God, and to enjoy the inheritance which Christ has purchased for us.

Secondly, the Law and covenant given by *Moses* is abolished in respect of the outward administration. Their obedience to the moral Law was first preached; and afterward the sacrifice of Christ was promised in types and figures. But now Christ is first preached, and then after justification in him, the Law is set as a rule to walk by in the way of sanctification; and also to show how it is impossible to find perfect righteousness, and to be justified and saved, but only in Christ. There the promises were set forth and sealed darkly in type and figure, but now these figures and ceremonies are ceased, and Christ the substance of them is set forth naked in his own colors before our eyes.

Thirdly, the covenant given by *Moses* may be said to vanish and be abolished in respect of the light and glory of it. For the light and glory of it, which it then had, is swallowed up of the great light of the Gospel. The glory of it was but like a dim light or candle, but the glory of the Gospel is like the light of the sun at noon day, so that before it the light of the Law is put out, and appears no more than the light of a candle in the bright sunshine. Now the apostle tells us, that, "When that which is perfect is come, then that which is in part is abolished," (1 Cor. 13:10). And in our common speech we say, that the brightness of the sun destroys and puts out the light of a candle, that it is as good as nothing; and so we may in the same sense say, that the covenant of the Law is abolished in respect of the light and glory of it; for the glory of it which was but in part is swallowed up by the great light of the glorious Gospel. But the covenant of the Gospel abides in all respects firm and sure forever, and we must never expect a plainer renewing of it to the end of the world. And so I have out of the Holy Scriptures, and especially from the words of the apostle discovered plainly the agreement and difference between the mixed covenant which God made with Israel by *Moses*, and the pure and simple Covenant of Grace with all nations in the Gospel, and published by Christ and his holy apostles and evangelists.

CHAPTER 17:

GOD'S PROVIDENCE

The use of the doctrine is shown for the discovering of God's singular providence in preparing means of grace fit for the several ages of the world.

The consideration of this discovers to us the singular providence of God in ordering the world, and his wonderful wisdom, goodness and mercy in preparing and giving means of grace and salvation fitted for the people of every age according to their several dispositions, and the necessity of every age and generation. In the first ages next to the state of innocency, when men lived diverse hundreds of years and had the helps of long observation and great experience, besides the instructions and historical relations of long-lived progenitors; who as eye and ear witnesses, could from *Adam, Methuselah,* and *Noah,* rehearse God's great works from the creation, and teach them the knowledge of God; then the Lord dealt more sparingly, and afforded but small and rare means, even a few visions, revelations, and general and obscure promises to turn men from their own ways, and draw them to seek salvation in him. But when men's ages and lives were shortened by the increase of corruption, and by men's multiplying of iniquity, and growing more hard, stubborn, and rebellious. The Lord, to the former promises made to the fathers, added a fiery Law which he gave from Mount Sinai, in thunder and lightning, and with a terrible voice to the stubborn and stiff-necked Israelites; whereby to break and tame them, and to make them sigh and long for the promised Redeemer, when they were pressed with the bondage of the Law, and with the intolerable burden of rites and ceremonies. And when after many ages they had grown desperately rebellious, that they scorned God's messengers, rejected his laws and commandments, misused and persecuted his extraordinary prophets, who worked wonders in their light, and killed his servants which he sent to them, then at last *he sent his Son* in whom he fulfilled all the promises made to the fathers. This Christ also fulfilled the Law both moral and ceremonial, and made reconciliations for sin and iniquity, and brought in eternal righteousness, and has made with all the world the New Covenant of the eternal Gospel of Peace, by which we receive the promise of the Spirit, who works in us all grace to the mortifying of the old man, subduing the rebellious flesh, casting down of the strongholds of sin and Satan, and bringing all thoughts in captivity to the obedience of Christ.

So as the world has had more need of stronger helps and powerful means, God in his *wise providence* has increased and supplied them in several ages; and as sin has more abounded, and stubbornness and hardness increased, so God has more showed his goodness, magnified his mercy, and enlarged his bounty, by giving more powerful means, by renewing and explaining the covenant of life and salvation, and making his grace more abound towards the sons of men. And therefore let us by this be stirred up to take notice of God's special providence, how he respects the sons of sinful men, and is mindful of them to visit them, and take care for them in all ages. Let us admire his wisdom, extol his goodness and mercy, and labor to bring forth abundance of fruit, according to the culture and until age, and the powerful means of grace which God has bestowed on us under the Gospel.

Let us be ashamed and confounded in ourselves, for our barrenness after so many plentiful showers poured down on us; and acknowledge and confess we had long ago been overgrown with all wickedness, and swallowed up of our sins and iniquities, if the Lord had not by the strong hand of his glorious Gospel, and his mighty and powerful Spirit shed forth plentifully through Jesus Christ in these last days, stopped the current of our sinful corruption, and stayed us from running headlong into destruction. As for them who in their great light of the Gospel, multiply their works of darkness, and make their sins and transgressions ascend up in great multitude like thick clouds towards heaven, and do hate and persecute the truth which shines to them, and love the darkness of errors more than the light of sound doctrine; let them know that their rebellion against the light deserves the reward of the mist and blackness of darkness forever; let them fear and justly suspect that they are the ground which the apostle speaks of, (Heb. 6:8), which when it has drunken in the rain which often comes on it, brings forth no good fruit, but thorns, briars, and stinking weeds which are poison, and therefore is rejected, and is near to cursing, whose end is to be burned. And just it is with God, that he should send such persons strong delusions, that they should believe the lies of the man of sin, and run after errors and heresies, that they all may be damned who have not received the love of the truth that they might be saved; but have taken pleasure in unrighteousness, as the apostle has foretold, (2 Thess. 2:11-12).

CHAPTER 18:

THE LAW AND THE GOSPEL

Of the Law and the Gospel, and the agreement and difference between them.

Now the last thing only remains, in other words, the description of the Law and the Gospel, and their agreement and difference. This may quickly be dispatched in few words, for their agreement and difference may easily be discerned by those things which have been already delivered; the only thing which is now necessarily to be touched, is the meaning of the words, and the diverse significations of them. These being made plain, it will appear that all the agreements and differences between them have been before fully laid open and expounded.

First, for the Law, it is in the original Hebrew Scriptures called תּוֹרָה *Torah*) a word derived of יָרָה *Horah*, which signifies to teach, to instruct, to admonish, and also to shoot forth arrows and darts; and so if we consider it according to the true notation of the name, by Law in Scripture may be understood any doctrine, work, or writing which teaches, instructs and admonishes men how they out to live, and how to walk before God, or among men, and any precept which as a dart or arrow is fastened in our hearts by our teachers.

But in the New Testament the Law is called νόμος (*nomos*) and is derived of a Greek verb which signifies to *distribute*, because the Law enjoins to distribute and give to God and men their due, and the revelation of the word and Law is God's distribution or dividing of his promises and his will among men. So then the word *law*, considered according to the natural sense of it in the original Scriptures of the Old and New Testament, may signify any doctrine, instruction, law, ordinance, custom, and statute human or divine, which teaches, directs, commands or binds men to any duty which they owe to God, or any of his creatures. And indeed so far the signification of it extends. For in Scripture it signifies, sometimes the special laws of heathen nations, as of the Medes and Persians, and the statutes and customs of men according to which they live among themselves, and their doctrines and instructions; but I omit the human significations of it, as not necessary for our present purpose; and I come to the divine which are diverse in Scripture.

First, this word *Torah* signifies, in a most large sense, any godly or profitable counsel, doctrine, instruction, or precept which parents give to their children, or one man to another, either by word or writing, which is not contrary, but according to the will of God and the rule of godliness, and serves to direct a man how to live or how to walk, either in his general or particular calling. So the word is often used in the Book of Proverbs, (Prov. 3:1, 4:2, 7:2). In which places the wise man exhorts his son to keep his Law, that is, all his precepts, counsels, and doctrines, and not to forget or forsake them.

Sometimes it signifies in a large sense, the whole doctrine of the word of God, which he has at any time revealed, or reveals in the whole Scriptures, both of the Old and New Testament; and so it includes the Law of *Moses*, the writings of the prophets, and all the evangelical promises made to us in Christ from the beginning; so it is used, in these words, "But his delight is in the Law of the Lord," (Psalm 1:2), and "The Law of the Lord is perfect, converting the soul," (Psalm 19:7), that is God's word, for the Law alone without the Gospel *cannot convert souls*, and Psalm 119 in diverse places where the Law is said to quicken, and to be the godly man's delight, and to comfort him in trouble.

Sometimes this word signifies only the Scriptures of the Old Testament, as John 15:25, where our Savior citing a speech out of Psalm 35:19, faith it is written in the Law, that is the Old Testament. And the apostle, 1 Cor. 14:21, repeating the words of *Isaiah*, (Isa. 28:11), says it is written in the Law.

Sometimes it signifies the whole doctrine of the five books of *Moses*, as "Let not the book of the Law depart out of thy mouth," (Josh. 1:7-8), and Luke 24:44, where our Savior distinguishes the Law, that is, the writings of *Moses* from the Psalms and the prophets. Also Matt. 12:5, John 7:23, and John 8:17, things written in the Book of Genesis as well as things written in the other four books are said to be written in the Law.

Sometimes the word *law* signifies in a more strict sense, the Doctrine of the Law, as it is different from the Doctrine of Grace, and is opposed to the plain Doctrine of the Gospel; that is, the whole sum of precepts, moral, ceremonial, and judicial, set down in the writings of *Moses*; so the word is used by the apostle in the epistles to the *Romans* and *Galatians*, where he opposes the Law and Doctrine of Works to the Gospel and Doctrine of Faith.

Sometimes by law in a most strict sense is meant, wither the moral Law contained in the Ten Commandments, as Exod. 24:12, or any of the ceremonial Laws, as the Law of the burnt offering, Lev. 6:9, the Law of sacrifice, Lev. 6:14, the Law of the sin offering, Lev. 6:24, or the judicial Law, and any precept of it, as Exod. 18:16 and Deut. 17:11.

Sometimes the word *Law* signifies the Doctrine of the Gospel, which as a new Law commands us to repent of all our sins, and to believe in Jesus Christ. So the word *Torah* is used, where the prophet says, "That in the last days the Law shall go forth our of Zion, and the word of the Lord from Jerusalem," (Isa. 2:3); meaning the publishing of the Gospel from there into all nations of the world; and the Gospel as it enjoins us to believe, is called the Law of Faith, (Rom. 3:27).

Sometimes the word *law* signifies the power, authority, and dominion, either of the flesh and the old man of sin dwelling in our member; or of the Spirit and new man ruling in the mind, where the apostle says, "I see another Law in my members, warring against the Law of my mind," (Rom. 2:7); that is, I see the power of sinful corruption, and of the old man striving against the Spirit, or part renewed, and "For the Law of the Spirit of life in Christ Jesus has freed me from the law of sin and death," (Rom. 8:2).

These are the diverse significations of the word *law*, which is called *Torah* in the Old, and *nomos* in the New Testament.

The word *gospel* is in the Hebrew text in the Old Testament called בְּשׂוֹרָה *Bessorah*, and in the New Testament εὐαγγέλιον (*euaggelion*) they both signify good news, glad tidings, and a joyful message; the one is derived of the Hebrew verb *Bissar* and the other of the Greek word εὐαγγελίζω (*euaggelizo*), which both signify one thing, namely to tell good news, or bring glad tidings. For the Greek word, it is diversely used in Scripture, and in other Greek authors.

Sometimes for the reward which is given to one for bringing good news, as 2 Sam. 4:10, where the reward which the man expected from *David* for the tidings of *Saul's* death is by the translators of the Septuagint called εὐαγγελιζόμενος, and in the Hebrew *Bessorah*. Sometime in heathen writers, the sacrifices which men offered up in thankfulness for the good news, as in *Xenophon lib. I Isocrates Areopage.*

Sometimes it signifies good news in general of what matter soever. David said of Ahimaaz, "He is a good man, he bringeth good tidings," (2 Sam. 18:27), the word is in the Hebrew *Bessorah,* and in the Greek εὐαγγελίζομαι, always signifies the *good tidings* and joyful message of Jesus Christ the Savior of the world, and of redemption by him, and so we always use the word Gospel in our English tongue; and when the word Gospel is so restrained to the message, and tidings of Christ, I find it used three ways in Scripture and in our common speech.

Sometimes it is opposed to the Doctrine of the Law which teaches to seek life and salvation by our own works, and then it signifies the whole Doctrine of Salvation by Jesus Christ, written in the Old and New Testament, and preached by all the ministers of Christ, to the end of the world, "God is my witness whom I serve with my Spirit, in the Gospel of his Son," (Rom. 1:9), and where the promise of Christ to *Abraham* is called the Gospel, (Gal. 3:8), and where the doctrine of believing and trusting in Christ is called the Gospel of salvation, (Eph. 1:13). In this large sense it includes all the promises of Christ in it which were made from the beginning to the fathers, before the Law, and by the prophets under the Law.

Sometimes it is opposed to all the promises of the Old Testament made to the fathers before the Law, and by the prophets before the coming of Christ, and then it signifies that joyful message; and word which is comprehended in the New Testament, which declares that Christ is already come in the flesh, and what he has done for our redemption, and how we must be brought to communion of life, and salvation in him. So it is used, where it is said, "that Jesus Christ preached in Galilee the Gospel of the kingdom of God," (Mark 1:14), and "Go preach the Gospel to ever creature," (Mark 16:15). When the word is so taken, it differs, and is distinguished from the promises of Christ to come which are called εὐαγγέλιον. It signifies Christ already come.

Sometimes this word is restrained to the written history of Christ, from his conception and birth, to his ascension, as it is recorded by the evangelists in the New

Testament; so the word is used, (Mark 1:1). Where the evangelist beginning his holy history says; the beginning of the Gospel of Jesus Christ; and so we use the word, when we speak of the Gospel of St. *Matthew*, or of *Luke*, or of *John*, meaning the history of Christ written by them.

Now having laid down the true signification of these two words, Law and Gospel, and showed the diverse acceptations of them, it is easy to gather the agreement and differences which are between them. If we take the word *Law* in the largest sense, for the whole word of God, then it includes the entire Gospel in it, and then they differ and agree as the whole body differs from, and agrees with a part of itself, the Law is the whole word of God, and the Gospel a part of it. If we take the Law for the Scriptures of the Old Testament, or for the writings of *Moses*, then it includes in it a *part* of the Gospel; namely, the promises of the Messiah, and the doctrine of salvation in him to come. And from the other part of the Gospel, in other words, the glad tidings of Christ already come, it differs as the Old Testament from the New, and the mixed covenant from the pure Covenant of Grace.

If we take the word *law*, for the new Law the Gospel of Grace, then the new Law and the Gospel are all one and the same. But if we take the Law for the Doctrine of Commandments, moral, ceremonial, and judicial, it differs from the Gospel so far as the first part of the covenant of God given by *Moses* differs from the pure Covenant of Grace. And lastly, if we by Law understand the moral, then it differs from the Gospel, so far as the first Covenant of Works differs from the second Covenant of Grace.

But if we take the Gospel in the most common and usual sense for the *glad tidings* of Christ already exhibited, and for the whole Doctrine of the New Testament, and by Law do understand (as the word commonly signifies) the covenant which God made with Israel by *Moses*, and the pure Covenant of Grace made with all nations, do agree and differ between themselves.

Now the use of these doctrines is manifold.

First, they serve to set us in a more sure way to salvation, and also to guide and keep us in this to the end, in that they show us every turning, and every by-way, both on the right hand and on the left, and how we may avoid them all. Many are the errors which have been raised up on the church of God from the first time of publishing of the Gospel until this day. In the time of the apostles, some taught that the Law was to be observed, together with the Gospel and the ministry of *Moses*, with the ministry of Christ, and that none could be justified or saved without circumcision and observation of the

Laws of *Moses*. Against them the apostle disputes in the whole epistle to the *Galatians*.

Some utterly destroyed the Law and all use of good works, and taught faith alone without works of sanctification at all. Against them the apostle *James* disputes. Some utterly rejected the Old Testament, as the Manicheans in old time, and now the Anabaptists. Some set up their own righteousness, as the Jews, (Rom. 10:3), and the papists at this day.

Now if we rightly understand the doctrines before laid down between the Old and New Covenant, the Law and the Gospel, we shall easily discern the wickedness of these errors, and shall see the right way to justification and salvation. We shall so understand the Scriptures of the Old and New Testament, that we shall out of them be able to answer all heretics and adversaries of the truth.

And therefore whatever some think of this discourse of the Old and New Testament, the first and the second covenant, mixed and pure Covenant of Grace; and concerning the Law and the Gospel, yet I am sure that others of better judgment, who receive with due respect and reverence all holy doctrine, shall find infinite profit, benefit, and comfort, if they *lay these things to heart,* and keep them in *continual remembrance.* Which grace the Lord grant to us all for his own mercy's sake in Jesus Christ. And I pray that this small work of a weak instrument will give a blessing to whose holy name is all praise an glory now and forever. *Amen.*

FINIS.